After September

A play

Jimmie Chinn

Samuel French — London
New York - Toronto - Hollywood

AFTER SEPTEMBER

First presented by the O.H.A.D.S. at The Garrick Studio Theatre, Hampton, Middlesex, on 29th November 1988, with the following cast:

Mr Smith	Colin Greenhalgh
Miss D'Vere	Marion Brazier
Miss McBain	Anne Low
Miss Fisher	Jackie Barrett
Miss Bickerstaff	Pamela Hickson
Miss Kershaw	Dorothy Jones
Miss Duke	Carol Ison
Miss Godfrey	Gwen Ransom
Miss Pink	Maggie Greenhalgh
Miss Cross	Mary Able
Miss Kyte	Eileen Nichols

Directed by Jimmie Chinn
Designed by Colin Greenhalgh
Lighting and Sound by Paul Greenhalgh

CHARACTERS

Mr Smith
Miss D'Vere
Miss McBain
Miss Fisher
Miss Bickerstaff
Miss Kershaw
Miss Duke
Mrs Godfrey
Miss Pink
Miss Cross
Miss Kyte

The action takes place in the staffroom of the Gwendolen Kyte School for Girls

Time — a day in September, in the early sixties

Mr Smith: Septimus. HMI, nondescript, 35-55.

Miss D'Vere: (teaches English). Has been at the school seven years. A smoker, close friend of Miss Duke. 30s.

Miss McBain: Phoebe (teaches chemistry). Scottish, waspish, precise in manner and appearance — faded. 50s.

Miss Fisher: Molly (teaches maths). Oldest member of staff. 60-plus.

Miss Bickerstaff: Dorothy (Deputy Head, matron, secretary). At the school 16 years. Hardworking, efficient. 40-plus.

Miss Kershaw: Kitty (teaches P.E.). At the school 20 years. Hearty, a "woman of the world". 40-plus.

Miss Duke: (teaches history/geography). Youngest member of staff, and the only one who wears trousers. Close friend of Miss D'Vere. Late 20s-30.

Mrs Godfrey: Vi (tea lady cum cook/cleaner). Common, funny. 50-plus.

Miss Pink: Rose (teaches music). At the school 18 years. Prim, fussy, small. 50-plus.

Miss Cross: Marjorie (teaches R.E.). Untidy, nervous, alcoholic. 40-50.

Miss Kyte: Ursula (Headmistress). Unhappy but capable of very dry humour, tired, grand. 60s.

The staff of the Gwendolen Kyte School for Girls are a curious bunch. They dress not in fashion, but in clothes of an earlier period (forties and fifties) in shades of brown or navy blue. They appear somehow other-worldly, belonging to another time and place.

To Maggie and Colin … thanks for all those Sundays

ACT I

*The staffroom at the Gwendolen Kyte School for Girls, somewhere in the
Home Counties. It is September, in the early Sixties*

*The room has a distinctly Forties feel: there is the usual collection of old
leather armchairs; an old horse-hair sofa with a book lying open on it; a
large table with a bag on it and covered with newspapers, magazines and
several piles of exercise books—all unmarked from the last term; a worn
carpet on the floor seems to define the acting area. There are two
entrances: one through double doors which lead out to a hall and
staircase, the other through french windows which lead out on to the
grounds of the house. The french windows stand open at all times*

In the darkness we hear a girls' choir singing "For All The Saints"

*After a moment, the Lights slowly come up, bathing the room in an autumn
glow, sun pouring in through the windows, leaving its shadows in the
corners*

The singing fades away

*Mr Smith is standing c. He looks about the room and its contents. He is
rather nondescript in his pin-striped suit, his bowler hat and bicycle clips.
In his hand, he holds his briefcase and umbrella. After a moment, he
removes the bicycle clips, puts them into his briefcase and brings out a
note-pad and a clipboard on which he begins to jot down the odd comment
on what he sees. His face is expressionless—it betrays nothing. A clock,
unseen in the hall, strikes three. Mr Smith checks his watch, makes a note
on his pad, then, taking his belongings with him, exits through the french
windows*

*Miss D'Vere enters from the hall. The only smoker on the staff, she has a
cigarette and carries an ashtray. She stops, looks about her as if sensing
a stranger. She calls*

Miss D'Vere (*puzzled*) Hallo?

No reply. She dismisses it and sits, feet up on the sofa. She picks up the book, reads and smokes

> *Miss McBain enters from the hall. She is wearing a tweed cape and a brown hat. She carries an old leather suitcase with straps, her bag and gloves—a study in shades of brown and tweed*

Miss D'Vere (*pleased to see her*) Phoebe, dear.

Miss McBain (*never one for intimacy*) Miss D'Vere. You look as if you'd been sitting there for ever.

Miss D'Vere Got back yesterday.

Miss McBain (*putting her luggage down*) This place reeks of cigarettes already.

Miss D'Vere (*with a big smile*) Me, dear—sorry.

Miss McBain At the end of last term you said you were giving it up. I thought it was too good to be true.

Miss D'Vere It's the will-power. I haven't any. Good holiday?

Miss McBain (*removing her hat*) Quite nice. I'm afraid it rained most of the time.

Miss D'Vere I thought it always rained in Edinburgh.

Miss McBain The rain is but scant price to pay for the peace and tranquillity of home, Miss D'Vere.

Miss D'Vere And Mother?

Miss McBain (*removing her scarf and gloves*) As usual—hale and hearty—but somewhat lonely, I suspect.

Miss D'Vere You should get her down here.

Miss McBain (*not wishing to pursue this topic*) Yes, well. And you?

Miss D'Vere The Dolomites.

Miss McBain Exotic.

Miss D'Vere Very.

Miss McBain Alone?

Miss D'Vere No. With Miss Duke.

Miss McBain I would have thought one wanted to get away from one's colleagues. Cooped up here for months on end. (*She moves to her pigeon-hole and looks through various coloured memos*)

Miss D'Vere Miss Duke and I have a lot in common.

Miss McBain (*reading a memo*) I see we're to have new classrooms again.

Miss D'Vere Yes. Outrageous. I'm going to complain.

Miss McBain A complaint to Miss Kyte is equal to a cry in the wilderness, I fear.

Miss D'Vere I know—but one can do it all the same.

Miss McBain Do we know the reason?

Miss D'Vere Apparently the ceiling in the East Wing fell down during the holidays. Bang goes our rise!

Miss McBain Nothing surprises me anymore. The place is so decrepit it's a wonder anything is left standing. (*She reads another memo*) I see there's to be an economy drive on chalk and pencils. She expects us to write in blood, I suppose.

Miss D'Vere I should sit down before you read the green one.

Miss McBain (*reading the green one*) My God!

Miss D'Vere I did warn you.

Miss McBain This is scandalous. Are we to have no privacy!

Miss D'Vere (*quoting*) "Owing to the unexpected lack of space ..."

Miss McBain (*reading*) "Owing to the unexpected lack of space, I'm afraid it will be necessary for you to share your sleeping quarters with Miss Pink. I'm sure, like us all, you will pull together in these difficult times, Ursula Kyte—Headmistress." Is it a joke?

Miss D'Vere A joke? Here?

Miss McBain And what, pray, does "pull together" mean? Well, I'm sorry, it's out of the question.

Miss D'Vere Dear Pink will have you up half the night practising your scales.

Miss McBain I refuse to share my bedroom with a musician. If anyone should share it's Miss Bickerstaff. She's had that large room to herself for far too long.

Miss D'Vere Not anymore, dear. She's having to bed down with old Molly Maths.

Miss McBain (*removing her cape*) It's almost obscene. Well, I shall have something to say about this!

Miss D'Vere (*enjoying it all*) A cry in the wilderness, dear—remember.

Miss McBain Of course, Headmistress Kyte remains where she is?

Miss D'Vere Of course.

Miss McBain And the girls? They're twelve to a dormitory as it is.

Miss D'Vere They're fine. Their ceilings are intact.

Miss McBain More than can be said for some of them after eight weeks on the loose. By the by, what news on Betty Bowker?

Miss D'Vere Banished! Forever. She and her child must now be educated by the State. Belmont Fields Secondary, I'm told.
Miss McBain Oh, dear. (*She moves to the window*)
Miss D'Vere We're in the Sixties now, Phoebe. Free love is dished out with the free milk.
Miss McBain (*staring through the window, world weary*) Well, at least she's escaped this place.
Miss D'Vere Cheer up, Phebs—soon be Christmas.
Miss McBain Every July I say that's it... Every autumn I'm back saying, "Ah, well, after September it'll be Christmas—then Easter". We wish our lives away.
Miss D'Vere Never mind. We could be nuns, dear. Look at the life they lead.
Miss McBain Nuns are lucky—at least they believe in something. And they don't have to share a bedroom with Rose Pink.
Miss D'Vere Seen the exam results?
Miss McBain (*expecting the worst*) Don't tell me.
Miss D'Vere They're excellent. All mine passed in English. Except Sylvia Twine.
Miss McBain Sylvia Twine should be in a home for the bewildered. The girl's a liability. (*She looks out into the garden*) At least the grounds are beautiful. Isn't it odd—there's nowhere like a school for making one aware of the impact of time. The seasons come and go—new girls arrive looking just like the old. Us. Getting older. (*She seems lost in time. Then she shades her eyes from the sun*) Who's that?
Miss D'Vere (*deep in her book*) What?
Miss McBain (*dismissing it*) Nothing—I thought I saw a stranger. (*She smiles*) Kitty's at it already out there. Running round the grounds jumping fences—strong as a horse. You know, I admire old Kitty. Always cheerful, never complains.
Miss D'Vere It's all that fresh air. (*She takes a drag on her cigarette*) I'm afraid it would choke me.

Miss Fisher enters looking bewildered. She is the oldest member of staff, short sighted, wearing half glasses. She wears an academic gown, and carries a pile of exercise books and her coloured memos

Miss Fisher (*alarmed*) I'm to share my room with Dorothy Bickerstaff!
Miss D'Vere Hallo, Molly. Welcome home.

Miss Fisher Did you hear what I said? I'm to share my-ten-by-eight mouse-hole with Dorothy Bickerstaff!

Miss D'Vere That's nothing, dear. Phoebe here's got Rose Pink.

Miss Fisher It can't be right. We'll have the sanitary man down on us like a ton of bricks.

Miss D'Vere Never mind—you'll have someone to cuddle up to at last.

Miss Fisher (*not amused*) I see—the smutty jokes have started already. Hallo, McBain. Nice holiday?

Miss McBain Well, it was a rest. A change from Hideaway Hall here.

Miss Fisher Mother?

Miss McBain Just the same.

Miss Fisher You should bring her down here—do her the world of good.

Miss McBain How was West Wittering?

Miss Fisher West Wittering was West Wittering. Had to cut it short. Doris had a slight stroke.

Miss McBain (*genuinely*) Oh, dear—I am sorry.

Miss D'Vere Your sister?

Miss Fisher Yes. Doris. Still, it gets us all in the end. Just thank God we have our jobs, eh?

Miss D'Vere Who'll look after her?

Miss Fisher I have another sister. Joan. She's retired from the Civil Service—she'll keep an eye on her, and I'll pop home whenever I can. (*She sits. Sadly*) Yes, there are the three of us—Joan and Doris and me.

Miss D'Vere Isn't that sweet? Three sisters. Sounds rather Chekhovian.

Miss Fisher Who?

Miss McBain Unless he was a mathematician, Molly won't have heard of him.

Miss Fisher (*showing a text book*) I found this in my pigeon-hole. *Maths and How to Teach It*. Bloomin' sauce! I suppose she put it there. Do you think it's a hint?

Miss D'Vere New publication, dear. Free sample. I got one. *English and the Backward Child*. Burn it. I did.

Miss McBain Miss D'Vere tells me the exam results were good.

Miss Fisher Thank God. All mine passed. All except Sylvia Twine, that is. (*She lowers her voice*) By the way—how is Betty Bowker?

Miss McBain Left, I fear. Under a cloud and heavy with child.

Miss Fisher Silly girl. She won't know one end of a baby from the other.

Miss McBain At least she's having a baby. More than can be said for any of us.

Miss Fisher (*shocked*) McBain!

Miss D'Vere Phoebe's down in the dumps, Molly. First day back and all that.

Miss Fisher Oh, I love first days back. The challenge—the sense of adventure—the smell of Mansion Polish and disinfectant everywhere. A new box of chalks—a new set of books to mark. (*She looks at her green memo*) Mind you, this has ruined everything. A lodger at my time of life. I shan't be able to wash my smalls in the sink anymore.

Miss D'Vere Why ever not? Even Miss Bickerstaff must wear knickers.

Miss Fisher You're trying to shock me, D'Vere—and I've made a new term's resolution: I refuse to be shocked. It's bad for my heart.

Miss Bickerstaff, harassed, enters in a hurry

Miss D'Vere Ah, Miss Bickerstaff—we were just talking about you.

Miss Bickerstaff You haven't seen a stranger in here, have you?

Miss Fisher (*holding up her green memo*) Miss Bickerstaff, I think we should discuss this.

Miss Bickerstaff (*not listening*) And I want the Head—I've searched everywhere—not a sign. It's all rather worrying.

Miss D'Vere She'll turn up, dear. She usually does.

Miss Bickerstaff I'm talking about him—I'm looking for a man.

Miss McBain Aren't we all, Dorothy. I gave up years ago.

Miss Bickerstaff (*on her way out again*) I've simply got to find him— I think we're in trouble.

She exits into the hall

Miss Fisher (*calling after her*) Bickerstaff, I refuse to have that dreadful dog in my room!

Miss D'Vere Too late—"the wind hath carried her abroad"!

Miss Fisher Even Bickerstaff I could get used to after a while—but the school dog is another story. It's rotting on its feet.

Miss McBain Do I sense a drama in the air?

Miss D'Vere And the girls aren't even back till tomorrow.

Miss McBain Poor Bickerstaff. At least we've had a holiday. She's probably been hard at it all summer.

Miss Fisher It's her fault if she chooses to work her fingers to the bone. She seems to think the place will fall down without her.

Miss McBain (*referring to the fallen ceiling*) It seems to manage that quite well on its own. (*She collects her things*) I'd better unpack before tea.

Miss Kershaw runs in from the garden, hot, breathless and already in her PE gear with white ankle socks and pumps

Miss Kershaw (*running once round the room, timing herself with a stopwatch*) Hiya, girls. That's it—up to scratch—twenty-four minutes—ten seconds. (*She flops down in her chair*) You know, I'm quite puffed though.
Miss D'Vere You look it. Aren't you too old for all that sort of thing?
Miss Kershaw Too old? Tosh. Sitting on your bum—smoking fifty fags a day—you'll be dead long before me. Hallo, Molly, love. (*To Miss McBain*) Maccers—nice time with Mum?
Miss McBain (*moving to the exit*) Very nice, thank you, Kitty. Excuse me—I must away.
Miss Kershaw Rose Pink's been trying to track you down and she's flushed with temper, whatever it is.
Miss McBain (*moving to the exit*) I know what it is. The green memos bear unwelcome news.

Miss McBain exits

Miss Kershaw Green memos? What's all that about?
Miss Fisher You must have had one. We all have.
Miss Kershaw Probably. Never read them. Old Kyte stirring up trouble again, is she?
Miss Fisher Some of us have to share—me with Bickerstaff, and Phoebe with Pink. It's un-natural.
Miss Kershaw Could be cosy. Those cold winter mornings can be hell out here.
Miss Fisher (*rising*) Yes, well, I must go and tidy my classroom for tomorrow. I start with lower fourth remedial. Turns your stomach, doesn't it?
Miss Kershaw How you can teach boring old maths anyway, beats me, Molly. (*To Miss D'Vere*) Or English, come to that.
Miss Fisher (*moving to the exit*) Someone has to, Kitty, someone has to. See you later.

Miss Fisher exits

Miss Kershaw (*throwing her legs over the arm of her chair*) She's a dear old thing—Molly Maths.

Miss D'Vere Her sister's had a stroke.

Miss Kershaw Is that right? Which one?

Miss D'Vere Doris.

Miss Kershaw Oh, dear. Poor old Molly. They've led her a dog's life, you know. Absolute dog's life. That's why she loves it here at Kyte's. At least here she's got her independence.

Miss D'Vere Not anymore.

Miss Kershaw I know—what a gas, eh? Well, at least they daren't shove anyone in with me. My room's so small you can rick your neck just putting your vest on. No change for you and Daphne, I suppose?

Miss D'Vere No—we're safe—thank God.

Miss Kershaw It's a rum old place this—have you ever thought? A lot of silly old women all shut up together. It can't be what the good Lord intended, can it?

Miss D'Vere We're not all old, Kitty, please.

Miss Kershaw Sorry, dear. No offence. You know what I mean, though. Like Molly said—it's un-natural.

Miss D'Vere I thought you enjoyed teaching.

Miss Kershaw I love it, dear. Absolutely love it. Well, the old physical training and that. Couldn't be stuck indoors like you lot. Drive me bonkers.

Miss D'Vere How long have you been here?

Miss Kershaw Don't ask, lovey, don't ask. I first came up that drive— must be—twenty years ago. Can you imagine that? Twenty years. I was just a slip of a thing in those days. Taught French, dear... French! Couldn't speak a bloody word of it. Old Gwendolen had gone into hospital—Ursula was up the creek—she took me on out of pure desperation. A mere pittance, mind. Low wages, my little boxroom in the attic, and sardines on toast for every meal. Who else would want a job like that?

Miss D'Vere You must have seen some changes.

Miss Kershaw Changes! Good God, no! Nothing much ever changes here at Kyte's. That's the reason we all stay. Take yourself for example. "She won't last long," we all said. Now look at you. How long?

Miss D'Vere This'll be my seventh year.

Miss Kershaw Seven years—is it really? And there you are, indistin- guishable from that sofa. I'll say this: you're a good teacher and the girls love you.

Miss D'Vere Do they? I can never tell.

Miss Kershaw Oh, I hear all sorts in that changing room. Who they like—who they don't.

Miss D'Vere Who don't they like? Go on, Kitty, tell me.

Miss Kershaw Mind your own business. What're you reading?

Miss D'Vere *Wuthering Heights.*

Miss Kershaw Can't be doing with it. Those dreary sisters should have been strangled at birth.

Miss Duke enters. She is the youngest member of staff, attractive, cheerful, and the only one who wears trousers

Miss Duke Got a shilling, D'Vere?

Miss D'Vere In my bag—on the table. What d'you want a shilling for?

Miss Duke The gas fire.

Miss D'Vere It's the middle of September.

Miss Duke (*going to the bag on the table*) In our room it is never the middle of September. I'm trying to unpack and it's freezing in there. Hallo, Kitty. Nice holiday?

Miss Kershaw Bloody awful. I loathe having nothing to do. You two?

Miss Duke (*getting a coin from Miss D'Vere's purse*) We loved it. All that lovely food. And the wine. Not to mention the sunshine, of course. You should try it sometime.

Miss D'Vere She's afraid of flying. Aren't you, dear?

Miss Kershaw Don't mind the flying—it's crashing that bothers me. (*She rises*) Ah, well, can't sit here all day.

Miss D'Vere Bridge this evening?

Miss Kershaw You're on. McBain's bound to join in. See you at the staff meeting—and high tea, of course.

Miss D'Vere (*smiling fondly*) Sardines on toast?

Miss Kershaw (*moving to the exit*) Shouldn't be surprised.

Miss Kershaw exits into the hall

There is at once an intimacy between Miss Duke and Miss D'Vere, an intimacy which, although present, is not pointed or overstated

Miss Duke (*after a pause*) All right?

Miss D'Vere I'm fine.

Miss Duke You're looking sad.

Miss D'Vere (*rising to look out of the window*) Am I? Not really. (*She pauses*) We don't lead a very exciting life, do we? (*She lights a cigarette*)

Miss Duke Nonsense. We've just been away—that was exciting. At Christmas you're coming home with me—that's exciting. Our girls passed their exams—what more could a teacher want?

Miss D'Vere I suppose so.

Miss Duke And we're safe. Tucked away here—in the middle of nowhere. With nice people.

Miss D'Vere (*looking out of the window*) They are nice, aren't they? You know, on holiday, I actually miss them. Even the odd ones—the funny ones.

Miss Duke Even you and I must seem "odd and funny" to someone. (*She pauses*) Come on—what is it?

Miss D'Vere Nothing—I told you—I'm fine.

Miss Duke I know you better than that. You're in your December mood. This is end-of-term talk and we haven't even started yet.

Miss D'Vere Do you think one day we'll become like them?

Miss Duke Perhaps we are already.

Miss D'Vere You're not. (*She turns and looks across at Miss Duke*) Why did you come here, anyway?

Miss Duke You've asked me that before. Hundreds of times.

Miss D'Vere You never answer.

Pause. They look at each other

Miss Duke (*reflectively*) There was an advert—on the notice board at college. It was smaller than the rest—less impressive, I suppose. I liked the sound of it. "Probationary teachers required to live in…" I took a bus—a Green Line… As we passed, I saw this rather neglected house through the trees with its Gothic windows and the ivy. The Gwendolen Kyte School for Girls—Private. It sounded ever so grand and other-worldly. (*She smiles*) I could see over the wall from the bus—there was Kitty with a group of girls. "Up, two, three, down, two, three!" she was shouting. I don't know what it was. I just knew I wanted to be here.

Pause. Miss D'Vere smiles at her and takes her hand for a moment

(*She rises*) Right. I must get on. (*She moves to the door*)

Miss D'Vere What're you doing?

Miss Duke Told you—unpacking. If it was left to you... (*She stops at the door*) By the way—have you any stamps?

Miss D'Vere In my drawer. Under the envelopes. (*Tactfully*) Who're you writing to?

Miss Duke I thought I'd drop a line to that nice couple we met at the hotel. They gave me their address as we left.

Miss D'Vere (*treading carefully*) Not Mr Newbury?

Miss Duke (*firmly*) Not Mr Newbury—no. And his name was Maurice.

The sound of clattering cups and saucers on a trolley breaks the intimate mood

Mrs Godfrey enters pushing a tea trolley. She is the school cook and cleaner, distinctly different from the rest of the women

Mrs Godfrey Don't ask! I'm doin' only what I'm told.

Miss D'Vere What's all this?

Mrs Godfrey "We'll have tea served in the staffroom, Mrs Godfrey", her Highness says. "Oh, yes, O mighty Queen", says I.

Miss D'Vere (*glancing at Miss Duke*) Oh, dear.

Mrs Godfrey (*parking her trolley, attending to cups, etc.*) There's trouble. Mark my words. Very big trouble. *She* hasn't been found yet, 'as she!

Miss Duke Found? Is someone lost, Vi?

Mrs Godfrey Trixie. She's gorn, in't she? Vanished! And I'm to blame, it seems.

Miss D'Vere (*puzzled*) Are you?

Mrs Godfrey Oh, yes, I'm to blame. Who else gets blamed for everything round here? "Don't think you can get away with this", she said to me last night.

Miss Duke Last night! You mean Trixie's been missing all day?

Mrs Godfrey Nobody's seen her since Gawd knows when. "I'm calling the coppers", she says.

Miss Duke What nonsense.

Mrs Godfrey Oh, she means it, miss. "If someone's murdered Trixie", she says.

Miss D'Vere Pure melodrama, Vi. Take no notice. People under stress often say things they don't mean.

Mrs Godfrey Under stress! I'm under stress. What with the ceiling down, my menus to fix, those buggers back tomorrow—but I don't go round calling people murderers!

Miss D'Vere Where is she now?

Mrs Godfrey Where she's been most of the morning—in the grounds—like a loony in her wellingtons looking for the body in the undergrowth.

Miss Duke and Miss D'Vere try hard not to laugh

If you ask me—old Bicker-knickers done her in. She was saddled with her, wasn't she?

Miss D'Vere And there was I—thinking the term was starting quite well.

Mrs Godfrey Don't you believe it, miss.

Miss Duke But she has no right to blame you, Vi.

Mrs Godfrey (*putting cups on saucers, spoons into saucers, wiping cups, etc.*) Try telling her that, miss. I've been accused before. Once when a silver spoon went missing, another time a leg of lamb—and last term a tin of treacle! Well, I can cope with all that. The spoon, the lamb and the treacle was my responsibility—that dog, I'm glad to say, is not!

Miss D'Vere Leave Miss Kyte to me, Vi. I'll have a word with her.

Mrs Godfrey I'd be ever so grateful if you would, miss. I mean, I've got a husband and a backward daughter at home—I can do without all this caper. And then there's that Pink woman screaming and carrying on all over the place.

Miss Duke Rose?

Mrs Godfrey She's refusing to budge. Supposed to move in with the chemistry woman, but she's making ever such a song and dance of it.

Miss D'Vere (*enjoying all the fuss*) Quite appropriate really—considering what she teaches.

Mrs Godfrey (*totally humourless*) What, miss?

Miss D'Vere Song and dance. Music?

Miss Duke D'Vere—stop it! So we think the dog is dead, Vi?

Mrs Godfrey I don't know what it is and I don't care. Ask me, it's been dead on its feet since old Mrs Kyte passed on—bless her. Now, there *was* a real lady—a proper headmistress—not like O Mighty One out there.

Miss Duke Miss Kyte is her daughter, Vi.

Mrs Godfrey So what? She's no more a teacher than I am, miss. Only took it on because of what it said in the will. She'd be rid of this place tomorrow, miss—mark my words. (*She lowers her voice*) If you ask me——

Miss Bickerstaff enters

Miss Bickerstaff I would have thought, Mrs Godfrey, with all the things you have to do, there'd be no time left for idle chit-chat.

Mrs Godfrey For your information, Miss Bickerstaff——

Miss Bickerstaff (*ignoring her*) I have instructions from Miss Kyte: she wishes the bell to be sounded in ten minutes, and all members of staff to assemble in here at once. Right?

Mrs Godfrey Ringing bells ain't my province—the girls usually do that.

Miss Bickerstaff The girls aren't here, Mrs Godfrey—the girls don't arrive until tomorrow. Now, choppity-chop!

Mrs Godfrey's voice trails away as she exits

Mrs Godfrey (*wiping her hands on her apron*) Do this—do that—I've a husband and a backward daughter at home, I'll have you know!

Miss Bickerstaff (*trying to remain calm*) If she once more mentions her backward daughter, I shall scream.

Miss D'Vere Poor Bickerstaff—how do you put up with all this? And why?

Miss Bickerstaff I do not need sympathy, Miss D'Vere—just everyone's co-operation.

Miss Duke (*leaving*) I'm off.

Miss Bickerstaff Ten minutes—in here, Miss Duke.

Miss Duke exits

Miss Duke (*off; calling*) I'll be there, don't worry.

Miss Bickerstaff Term has begun, Miss D'Vere.

Miss D'Vere Term has begun, Miss Bickerstaff. There's been a calamity, I hear.

Miss Bickerstaff Really? Which one? The fallen ceiling—the lack of suitable accommodation—the fact that no food has yet been delivered—or that at least twenty girls have not yet paid for the coming term? I have a catalogue of calamities.

Miss D'Vere I meant the disappearance of the dog.

Miss Bickerstaff The dog is no concern of mine. Personally, I shall be glad to see the back of it. Now, if you don't mind...

Miss Pink enters, distraught and angry

Miss Bickerstaff turns to leave, but runs into Miss Pink

Miss Pink Miss Bickerstaff!

Miss Bickerstaff Miss Pink.

Miss Pink I wish to complain.

Miss Bickerstaff If you would care to visit my office—shall we say six-fifteen?

Miss Pink Six-fifteen won't do, Miss Bickerstaff—six-fifteen will be too late—by six-fifteen I shall be hanging from the rafters in the Great Hall, and when they come to cut me down and enquire why a teacher of music should put so sudden and untimely an end to herself, I hope you will tell them that for eighteen years she had to endure every humiliation thrust upon her in this so-called academy of learning, but that the last straw, the final degradation, that of being turned out of her room—was just too much!

Miss Bickerstaff Miss Pink if, I could——

Miss Pink (*in full flow*) Life without a room to one's self is the ultimate insult, Miss Bickerstaff. And how you could even imagine that I would share a room with Miss McBain—a woman who hasn't spoken two words to me in all the years we've been here, is beyond my comprehension. I would rather sleep in the coal cellar with the rats and the mice!

Miss Bickerstaff Have you finished?

Miss Pink Yes!

Miss D'Vere (*applauding*) Good for you, Rose.

Miss Pink And I will not be made fun of, Miss D'Vere.

Miss D'Vere I'm not making fun—I'm applauding your courage, dear.

Miss Pink I need no applause—this is not a performance. I speak in earnest and I demand action. Even my classroom is in a different place.

Miss Bickerstaff As I explained in my blue and green memos, neither your bedroom or your classroom are safe, since both are in the East Wing, and the East Wing is dangerous.

Miss Pink And what about your room? It's large enough to drive horses through.

Miss Cross creeps in from the garden, unnoticed. She seems to be searching for something—lifting cushions, looking under chairs, etc. She is a sad and lonely woman, shabby and unkempt with ill-fitting clothes and a shiny face

Miss Bickerstaff If you'd taken the trouble to glance at the chart in the hall, you would have seen that my room is to become a new classroom and that I am to move in with Miss Fisher. So you see, Miss Pink, even I am affected by this hoo-hah.

Miss Pink Well, I'm going to write to someone in authority. I'm going to expose this school and its appalling inadequacies to the world!

Miss Bickerstaff (*with darker and deeper meaning*) Are you sure you haven't done that already?

Miss Pink And what is that supposed to mean?

Miss Bickerstaff We'll see—shall we? And now, if you'll excuse me— I have things to do.

Miss Bickerstaff exits

Miss Pink (*flushed pink*) What did she mean by that?

Miss D'Vere (*singing*)   "Happy days are here again—
                                   The skies above are clear again..."

Miss Pink looks askance and exits

Miss D'Vere laughs and returns to her book

Miss Cross pops up from behind the sofa

(*Suddenly aware of her*) Oh, my God! (*She puts her hand to her heart*) Marjorie—I didn't see you come in.

Miss Cross (*absorbed in the search*) Erm?

Miss D'Vere Are you all right, dear?

Miss Cross (*searching elsewhere*) Oh, yes.

Miss D'Vere Can I help?

Miss Cross (*still looking*) No, no. It's me. I'm so careless. I seem to have mislaid my knitting bag.

Miss D'Vere Oh dear.

Miss Cross You know the one—I often have it with me—large canvas thing.

Miss D'Vere A sort of dirty brown?

Miss Cross That's it. It's got my cardigan in it.

Miss D'Vere Cardigan? (*She looks for it*)

Miss Cross Yes, I thought I'd knit myself one. There was a pattern in *Woman's Own*. Never mind—it's obviously not here.

Miss D'Vere When did you last have it?

Miss Cross Let me think… It must have been the last day of term.

Miss D'Vere *Last* term! Oh, well. Could be anywhere, dear.

Miss Cross (*giving up the search*) Yes. I expect so. I'm sorry to cause such
a fuss over nothing. (*She turns to leave by the windows again*)

Miss D'Vere Nice holiday?

Miss Cross (*vaguely*) Sorry?

Miss D'Vere Holiday?

Miss Cross Oh, yes. The usual—you know…

Miss Cross exits into the garden

A handbell starts ringing very loudly out in the hall

Miss D'Vere (*putting her hands to her ears*) What the hell?

Mrs Godfrey enters ringing the handbell in a temper

Vi—please. (*Louder*) Vi!

Mrs Godfrey stops ringing the bell

What are you doing, dear?

Mrs Godfrey She said "Ring the bell"—so I'm ringing the bell. (*She
makes for the exit*) "Lovely fresh ices—get your ices here—lovely fresh
ices…"

She exits

Miss D'Vere (*to herself*) This is a madhouse!

*Miss McBain enters, covering her ears. She is now dressed in her white
working coat and rubber gloves*

Miss McBain Is there a fire or what?

Miss D'Vere I'm afraid Vi's in a mood.

Miss McBain There'll be another ceiling down if she's not careful. We
are to foregather, I'm told.

Miss D'Vere Yes, instructions from on high.

Miss McBain (*removing her rubber gloves*) Well, at least my chemistry

lab is in the same place. Under an inch of dust and some of my bottles
have been disturbed—but apart from that...

Miss D'Vere Poor Marjorie's back—looking as vague as ever.

Miss McBain Oh, dear. Why she sticks it is beyond me. The girls make
fun of her—her classes are forever in disorder. And having to teach
religious knowledge in this day and age—poor woman.

Miss D'Vere You're not fond of religion, are you?

Miss McBain I'm a scientist, Miss D'Vere—I like to have proof. I've no
time for myths or fable.

Miss D'Vere You enjoy assemblies—I've seen you.

Miss McBain Oh, I do. I enjoy a good sing-along. (*She sits*) In fact, music
is the only thing left that moves me. Music, that is, not musicians.
They're a strange set. (*She pauses*) You know, I went to a concert in
Edinburgh during my holiday. Brahm's *Requiem*. I sat there—Mother
by my side as usual—and I cried.

Silence

I actually wept. (*She lowers her head, overcome, ashamed. She weeps
softly to herself*)

Miss D'Vere (*sorry for her, understanding*) I know.

Miss McBain (*getting a hanky from her pocket*) I'm so sorry. I can't
think... (*She wipes her nose*)

Miss Fisher enters carrying books

Miss McBain turns away and pulls herself together

Miss Fisher (*bewildered*) Now I can't find my classroom. What is going
on, D'Vere?

Miss D'Vere Bickerstaff's done a chart.

Miss Fisher So I'm told—but I can't even find that. And why are we
meeting so early—is there an emergency?

Miss D'Vere Isn't there always?

Miss Fisher (*sitting in her chair*) Why we have to move at all is beyond
me. I was perfectly happy where I was.

Miss McBain (*herself again*) It's up to us to complain, but we never do.

Miss D'Vere Except Rose Pink—she's had a go at——

Miss Pink enters

Miss Pink Thank you, Miss D'Vere—if tales have to be told, I'll do the telling, if you don't mind. Miss McBain, I've been trying to locate you.

Miss McBain I haven't exactly been hiding, Miss Pink.

Miss Pink It has to be said—and it has to be said now—under no circumstances whatsoever could I possibly move in with you.

Miss McBain (*rising and moving to her own seat*) I'm just as unhappy about it. We shall just have to speak to Miss Kyte at this meeting. (*She sits*)

Miss Pink Precisely. (*She sits in her chair*)

Miss Kershaw runs in, breathless

Miss Kershaw Hallo, girls. Good to hear the old bell again, what? Ting-a-ling, and we all rush to get at it. Just like one of Pavlov's dogs. (*She laughs*)

No-one else laughs

Oh, dear—do I hear thunder?

Miss McBain Term has begun, Kitty.

Miss Bickerstaff enters, loaded with fresh papers, charts, etc.

Miss Bickerstaff Good-afternoon, ladies. Thank you for your promptness. As you will see from the trolley, tea will be served as we chat. May I? (*She starts to give out various sheets of paper to everyone*)

Miss Fisher Not more wretched bumf, surely. I'm swamped as it is.

Miss Bickerstaff Timetables, times of assemblies, form lists, inter-house activities——

Miss D'Vere Guides to family planning.

They all look at Miss D'Vere, unamused

Sorry.

Miss Duke enters, carrying two letters for the post

Miss Duke Family planning? Oh, I say, have I come to the wrong shop? Has the last post gone, Dorothy?

Miss Bickerstaff (*still handing papers round*) Five-thirty. You should know that by now, Miss Duke.

Miss Duke Oh, good. (*She holds up her two letters*) Could you?

Miss Bickerstaff (*taking the letters*) Thank you. (*She hands Miss Duke her share of papers*) Thank you.

Miss Duke Not more lists. (*She sits in her chair*)

Miss Bickerstaff Now, the Head will be here shortly, and I think it only fair to warn you that the last few days have been very trying for her. And for me. We don't all get a summer holiday, you know.

Miss Fisher Whose fault's that?

Miss McBain And we only get a small retainer fee, Dorothy.

Miss Bickerstaff (*sitting at the table*) If Miss Kyte could afford to pay you more, I'm sure she would. Now, may I finish?

Miss Kershaw Press on, Dorothy—get to the crunch, dear.

Miss Bickerstaff (*spreading her lists out on the table*) I was going to say, it would be wise, at least until after September, to treat Miss Kyte with kid gloves. Once the autumn term is under way, our own petty problems seem to get swallowed up by those of the pupils, no? (*She awaits a reply*)

No-one replies

Quite. So, if I may suggest, "gently be the path we tread"?

Miss Fisher What's that mean?

Miss D'Vere Shakespeare, Molly.

Miss Fisher He seems to have said everything, doesn't he?

Mrs Godfrey appears at the doors with an enormous enamel teapot

Mrs Godfrey Stand by your beds—her Ladyship's here!

Mrs Godfrey goes over to her trolley. The rest all stand, except Miss Pink who seems to wish to protest

Miss Kyte enters importantly. She has a dog's lead in her hand

Mrs Godfrey, unseen by the headmistress, curtsies deeply and, thumb to her nose, makes a rude gesture

Miss Kyte Good-afternoon, ladies.

All (*except Miss Pink*) Good-afternoon, Headmistress.
Miss Bickerstaff (*in a frantic whisper*) Miss Pink!
Miss Pink I refuse to enter into this charade.
Miss Kyte (*sitting in her seat*) You may sit, ladies, thank you.

Everyone sits. Mrs Godfrey stands by her trolley

Are we unwell, Miss Pink?

Miss Pink I am perfectly well, Headmistress. What I am not, however, is happy.

Miss Kyte Happy? Do you say "happy"? We are teachers, Miss Pink—we were not put upon this earth to be happy. I haven't been happy since nineteen forty-nine, but, like us all, I forge ahead. I realize, as I hope do the rest of you, that Kyte's is not a fun palace, a holiday camp by the sea, but a school—a vocation.

Miss Pink I do not need to be reminded, Headmistress. I have been here for eighteen years.

Miss Kyte Indeed. And always of great value to the school, Miss Pink. Your *Gondoliers* was the talk of the Home Counties. (*Acidly*) Your *Mikado* a little less so, but we won't go into that.

This is a wounding blow to Miss Pink. She flinches as if in pain, flushes, and is silent

Now, are we to know the cause of this unhappiness—or might it wait for Any Other Business?

Miss Pink (*wounded*) It can wait. (*She blows her nose*)

Miss Kyte Good. You may serve tea, Mrs Godfrey. I'm sure we must all be parched.

Mrs Godfrey (*pouring tea*) I did order a dozen fancies but the man with the van didn't turn up.

Miss Kyte Still no food, Miss Bickerstaff?

Miss Bickerstaff I've been on the phone twice. We can but hope, Headmistress.

Miss Kershaw Does this mean we get no supper, Vi?

Mrs Godfrey (*still pouring*) Oh, supper's okay—I've got some nice sardines on toast.

Miss Kershaw (*to herself*) Oh, good. That'll make a change.

When ready, Mrs Godfrey starts handing out the cups, to Miss Kyte first.

Miss D'Vere still has her feet up on the sofa

Miss Kyte (*to Miss D'Vere*) Quite cosy, are we, Miss D'Vere?
Miss D'Vere (*missing the sarcasm*) Quite cosy, thank you, Miss Kyte.
Miss Kyte Now, ladies—went our holidays well?

The ladies mumble various responses to her question

Miss Cross enters and tries to steal in unnoticed to her seat

Miss Kyte Are we playing games again, Miss Cross?
Miss Cross (*flushed*) I'm sorry?
Miss Kyte You entered so quietly, and so long after the bell, I wondered
 if we were to pretend you weren't here? (*She smiles slightly to Miss
 Cross*)
Miss Cross (*embarrassed*) Oh, I see. No, no. I was trying to avoid a fuss.

Miss Bickerstaff hands some papers to Miss Cross

Miss D'Vere Did you find it, Marjorie?
Miss Cross (*preoccupied with the papers*) I'm sorry?
Miss D'Vere (*to the others*) Miss Cross is bagless. She's had her knitting
 bag stolen.
Miss Kyte Stolen? Here at Kyte's? Surely not.
Miss Cross Oh, no. I seem somehow to have mislaid it. I'm sure it will
 turn up.
Miss Kyte (*stirring her tea*) Have we ginger nuts, Mrs Godfrey?
Mrs Godfrey No ginger nuts—sorry. (*She is not sorry at all*)
Miss Kyte (*at length*) Now, ladies. If I may, and before Dorothy
 Bickerstaff belabours us with her coloured lists—I have some very sad
 news.

A hush falls. They all look at Miss Kyte

Miss Pink (*very worried*) Not… Not Miss Finch?
Miss Kyte No, not Miss Finch. Miss Finch, I am happy to report, seems
 to be doing very well at the sanatorium. She appears to have stopped
 setting fire to things and I've sent her some flowers on our behalf. (*She
 pauses*) No, my news is not as joyful as that of Miss Finch. (*She holds
 the dog lead aloft*) You see what I have in my hand?

Miss Fisher Is it a whip?

Miss Kyte It's my little Trixie's lead. But as you can see—no little Trixie.

Mrs Godfrey (*with an edge to her voice*) Yes, we did notice that.

Miss Kyte Thank you, Mrs Godfrey—you may leave us now.

Mrs Godfrey (*sitting by her trolley*) No, thank you. If there's news of the animal I'd like to hear it.

Miss Kershaw Are we to take it Trixie has run off?

Miss Kyte (*scornfully*) "Run off", Miss Kershaw… Trixie would never "run off"!

Miss Fisher She is rather ancient.

Miss Kyte My mother was ninety when she died, Molly. But she wasn't in the habit of running off.

Miss Fisher (*puzzled, the logic of this escapes her*) I'm sorry, Ursula, I thought we were talking about a dog.

Miss Kyte You implied that great age brings with it a desire to flee from home. I'm saying Trixie would never do that. She loved it here at Kyte's—Kyte's was her home for the last twenty years.

Miss Kershaw And yet you speak of her in the past tense, Headmistress.

Miss Kyte (*darkly*) Yes. I wonder why? Perhaps it's a sixth sense that makes me suspect that perhaps she's been disposed of.

There is a dreadful hush—even the odd sharp intake of breath. They all look suspiciously at each other

Miss Fisher (*innocently*) It can only be a blessing, surely. She smelt to high heaven and could barely move about.

Miss McBain How long has she been gone, Miss Kyte?

Miss Kyte She was last seen… Miss Bickerstaff?

Miss Bickerstaff Five-thirty last evening. When I went down to the post-box. I was going to take her with me—I usually do.

Miss Kyte (*having heard all this before*) And?

Miss Bickerstaff But this time she seemed exhausted.

Miss Kyte Jaded, Miss Bickerstaff—weary.

Miss Bickerstaff Well—tired anyway. So I let her be. She was where she always was—on the end of my bed on the rug provided. And that's where I left her.

Miss Kyte But?

Miss Bickerstaff (*hanging her head*) I did leave my door open.

Miss Kyte (*rising and moving among them*) So you see, she must have popped out—come down here out through those windows—and out into the grounds to do her little jobs. And since? (*She pauses dramatically*) Not a sign. Gone. Vanished!

Miss D'Vere You speak almost accusingly, Headmistress.

Miss Kyte You came back yesterday, Miss D'Vere?

Miss D'Vere I did.

Miss Kyte And you, Miss Duke?

Miss Duke Yes.

Miss Kyte Miss Kershaw?

Miss Kershaw I came back last night to avoid the early morning traffic. Why?

Miss Kyte So, on the premises last evening were: myself as always, Dorothy Bickerstaff, Miss Duke and Miss D'Vere, Mrs Godfrey in her pantry, and Kitty Kershaw. (*She pauses*) And one other.

They all look at each other. Silence

Miss Cross?

They look at Miss Cross

I saw you last night, did I not? Quite late, in fact. Skulking in the shadows by the old well in the grounds.

Miss Cross (*embarrassed*) I can't imagine that I was "skulking". I often take a short walk in the grounds before bed. I'm sorry—but what is all this about?

Miss Fisher (*firmly*) Quite right, Marjorie. You are being a little heavy-handed, Ursula. You're making it sound as if one of us had deliberately put an end to your wretched dog.

Miss Kyte I merely wish to ascertain if anyone actually saw Trixie before her mysterious disappearance.

Miss Fisher You see—there you go again. Why should it be mysterious? The dog was older than God—it was bound to die sometime.

Miss Kyte Ah, so even you think it dead.

Miss Fisher I didn't mean that. I meant we should just forget it for the moment and get on with more important matters.

Miss Kyte (*taking offence, dismissively*) Right then—we'll just forget it. We'll try to forget that my poor mother's devoted pet has simply vanished into the night. We'll forget she ever existed, shall we? (*She sits*)

Everyone is slightly embarrassed by this performance

Miss Bickerstaff—to business, please.

Miss Bickerstaff (*confused*) Now?

Miss Kyte Now, Miss Bickerstaff, now!

Miss Bickerstaff (*consulting her lists*) Yes, well… Let me see… First on my list then—as Miss Finch is still unfit and unable to return to her duties—I shall remain as titular Deputy Headmistress, as well, of course, as remaining school secretary—and matron.

Miss Kershaw (*under her breath*) You deserve a medal, dear.

Miss Bickerstaff As you will see from your pink sheet, Betty Bowker will not be returning this term or, indeed, ever again. We did receive a most spiteful letter from her mother—very unkind and quite uncalled for. It's in my office if anyone would care to——

Miss Kyte That dog was my mother's pride and joy.

They all pretend not to hear this

Mrs Godfrey (*wanting to escape*) Well, I'd best get on with supper then. Six o'clock as usual?

No reply. The tension is great

Mrs Godfrey exits into the hall in haste

Miss Bickerstaff (*pressing on bravely*) Now, your blue sheets—there will be twenty-two new girls this term——

Miss Kyte I shouldn't be surprised if Mother's turning in her grave.

Miss Bickerstaff —and the new form will be taken by Miss Pink——

Miss Pink When I can find my new classroom!

Miss Bickerstaff The names of the new pupils are: Lucy Armatage, Christine Dolan, Audrey——

Miss Kyte (*irritated*) Surely we can all read, Miss Bickerstaff!

Miss Bickerstaff (*unnerved*) Yes, Miss Kyte, I'm sorry.

Miss Kyte (*rising*) I shall go to my room if no-one minds. I have the most frightful headache. Please inform me of any unexpected event. (*She moves to the exit*)

Mr Smith enters, barring her way out

Mr Smith Miss Kyte? Miss Ursula Phyllis Kyte?

Miss Kyte (*to Miss Bickerstaff*) Who is this person?

Mr Smith (*presenting her with a card*) My name is Smith, madam. Septimus Smith. I am one of Her Majesty's Inspectors for Education.

Miss Kyte What do you want with us?

Mr Smith I regret to inform you we have received a number of complaints about your school.

Miss Kyte (*bewildered*) Complaints? About Kyte's? *Dismissive sarcastic*

Mr Smith (*consulting his clipboard*) According to our sources, your school is: outmoded, old-fashioned, substandard, overcrowded, insanitary and unsafe.

Miss Kyte Outmoded? Insanitary?

Mr Smith Furthermore, I have it on good authority that not only are your staff grossly underpaid but that at least two are well beyond the age of retirement and at least another two unqualified for the tasks they perform.

Miss Kyte (*in shock*) Unqualified... Tasks...?

Mr Smith And finally—a drunk—a lunatic—and other persons whose characters are unspeakably flawed, are present on your staff. Have you anything to say, madam?

There is a dreadful hush

Miss Kyte Yes. I have. Your informant seems to have left something out. We also have a murderer in our midst. Miss Bickerstaff—deal with this person!

Miss Kyte exits

Black-out

In the darkness we hear the girls' choir loudly singing "All Things Bright And Beautiful"

As rapidly as possible, all the teachers exit taking their cups and their papers with them

Mr Smith sits at the table, and lays his own papers out before him

The singing fades as the Lights come up

It is early evening, the same day. A clock, unseen, strikes six

> *Mrs Godfrey enters to remove her trolley and collect any cups that have been left*

She creeps about, trying not to make a sound, but with an inquisitive eye on Mr Smith as he works quietly at the table

Mrs Godfrey (*after a pause, in hushed tones*) Excuse me, sir…

He continues to work, not even looking up

  Sir…?

Mr Smith (*without looking up*) Yes?

Mrs Godfrey Sorry to disturb you—you don't mind if I clear my trolley?

Mr Smith It makes no difference to me. (*He looks up*) Miss…?

Mrs Godfrey (*with a slight curtsey*) Godfrey, sir. Mrs. You been called in, have you? Sort of inspecting, are you?

He does not reply

  (*Two-faced*) Not before time, ask me. There's things going on here— well, the least said. But I've often said to my husband, "if only half them parents knew what I know"—and that Miss Kyte! Mean as a butcher's dog. Not a bit like her old mum.

He looks up at her with a steely gaze

  Yes, well… I'll push off then.

> *Miss Bickerstaff enters, harassed*

Miss Bickerstaff Mrs Godfrey, are the staff to get their supper or not? The hour has struck!

Mrs Godfrey (*pushing the trolley to the door*) Just coming. I was having a quiet word with the inspector here. (*She winks twice*)

Miss Bickerstaff Have you developed a nervous twitch, Mrs Godfrey? Your business is in the kitchen.

Mrs Godfrey Will you be stopping for a bite of supper, sir? Sardines. Very tasty and nutritious.

Mr Smith No, thank you. I have my sandwiches.

Mrs Godfrey exits, pushing her trolley

Miss Bickerstaff (*firmly*) Now, look here, Mr...
Mr Smith (*very calmly*) Smith—Septimus Smith.
Miss Bickerstaff It's all very well to barge in here without an invitation...
Mr Smith (*looking through papers*) We did write—twice. We did
  announce that I would be coming, Miss...
Miss Bickerstaff (*disarmed*) I'm sorry?
Mr Smith It's going to be much easier if I know who everyone is and what
  they do. (*He attempts a smile, but smiles are not in his nature*)
Miss Bickerstaff My name is Bickerstaff. Dorothy Maureen Bicker-
  staff—Deputy Headmistress while our Miss Finch is away.
Mr Smith Away?
Miss Bickerstaff Away, yes. Ill. In hospital.
Mr Smith (*writing it down*) I see. And you're wrong to assume I'm here
  without invitation, Miss Bickerstaff. When my office receives a com-
  plaint it is our duty to investigate.
Miss Bickerstaff (*uneasily*) Investigate? But what is there to investigate?
  What have we done?
Mr Smith (*not answering this*) Am I right in thinking your duties stretch
  far beyond those of a Deputy Headmistress, and that in fact you are also
  matron, secretary and accountant all rolled into one?
Miss Bickerstaff I suppose I am a sort of general factotum, yes. What
  of it?
Mr Smith Overworked and very much underpaid, I imagine.
Miss Bickerstaff Money holds no interest for me. I love my job and I love
  the school. Kyte's is my life.
Mr Smith Most admirable, I'm sure. But might one enquire for which of
  these duties are you actually qualified?
Miss Bickerstaff (*warily*) I'm sorry?
Mr Smith Qualified, Miss Bickerstaff. You do know what the word
  means?
Miss Bickerstaff (*losing ground*) I, er... Well...
Mr Smith (*looking through his papers*) You see, search as we may, we
  can find no actual record that you ever trained as a teacher, for example.

She begins to fidget and becomes flushed

Mr Smith And yet, I have it on good authority that, even with your astonishing ubiquity, you are often called upon to teach as well.

Miss Bickerstaff When a member of staff is indisposed I have been known to stand in—yes.

Mr Smith For which subject would that be?

Miss Bickerstaff For all subjects. Any subject. Kyte's has always been famous for an across-the-board education.

Mr Smith And your training as a nurse—where did you receive that?

Miss Bickerstaff Applying bandages to cuts and bruises and dealing with the bodily functions of a growing girl need no training—simply common sense.

Mr Smith And the skills of accountancy, Miss Bickerstaff. Where did you acquire those? (*He pauses*) You do do the school's accounts—the tax man may wish to know these things.

Silence. She is beaten. She sits

Miss Bickerstaff (*after a pause; quietly*) I qualified as a shorthand typist just before I came to the school.

Mr Smith (*writing it down*) I see.

Miss Bickerstaff (*raising her head, more defiantly*) All this is irrelevant, surely. (*Proudly*) I am self-taught. In all my sixteen years here I have learned to do everything—and do it well. I'm as good a teacher, nurse and accountant as the next man. Furthermore, I can, when Mrs Godfrey has one of her tantrums, produce eggs on toast for the entire school.

Mr Smith But you have no degree, Miss Bickerstaff, no diploma—no piece of paper to prove all this.

Miss Bickerstaff But that is nonsense. Do we ask the surgeon before he cuts—or the dentist before he drills—for their pieces of paper? (*She becomes heated*) The proof of my capabilities—my knowledge—my expertise is in the way I do my job—and I do my job superbly, Mr Smith!

Mr Smith (*calmly*) Losing our temper isn't going to help us. The point is—if I were so minded—I could have you out of this school by tomorrow—or at least back to your typewriter.

Miss Bickerstaff (*pale, shaken*) Is that what you're going to do?

Mr Smith It won't be necessary. After September, I doubt there will even be a school. (*He continues to write*)

Miss Bickerstaff But, surely—you speak in jest.

Mr Smith I'm afraid not.

Miss Bickerstaff But the school has been here for over sixty years.

Mr Smith We are aware of that, Miss Bickerstaff. But when it was founded by Gwendolen Kyte all those years ago, she had twenty pupils. You now have many more than that—in a building that has never been enlarged or repaired or even passed as safe by the local fire department. You are behind the times, Miss Bickerstaff—the place is not only a health hazard but a death-trap.

Silence. She rises and moves across to the windows, with her back to him, and looks out. She is stunned. He watches her for a moment

(*With a hint of kindness*) I'm not a heartless man, Miss Bickerstaff. I can see what all this means to you.

Miss Bickerstaff (*quietly to herself*) Can you? I wonder.

Mr Smith May I, with respect, suggest that all of this is Miss Kyte's problem—not yours.

Miss Bickerstaff I'm afraid she's locked herself away in her room. She often does that.

Miss Duke enters quietly

Miss Duke May I come in? Are you all right, Dorothy?

Pause

Dorothy?

Miss Bickerstaff (*turning, wiping her nose, hiding her tears*) Ah, Miss Duke. This is our Miss Duke—history and geography. And fully qualified in both.

Miss Duke They sent me to fetch you, Dorothy. OK?

Miss Bickerstaff I shall be fine.

Miss Duke (*going to her; concerned*) You look awful. (*To him*) What have you been saying to her?

Mr Smith Simply that this school is a mess, Miss Duke, and must be closed without delay.

Miss Bickerstaff (*leaning on Miss Duke*) I feel rather unwell.

Miss Duke Of course you do, dear. Why not go into the dining-room with the others and have something to eat?

Miss Bickerstaff Yes. Yes, perhaps I shall.

Miss Bickerstaff exits quietly into the hall

Miss Duke (*angrily*) Look, who are you?

Mr Smith (*writing calmly*) I have my credentials if you wish to see them.

Miss Duke You can stick your credentials... I don't want you intimidating my colleagues—right? Whatever's wrong with this place has nothing to do with us. It's Ursula Kyte's business.

Mr Smith I agree. But Miss Kyte is locked away in her ivory tower.

Miss Duke You can tell me one thing—who betrayed us? Was it a member of staff?

Mr Smith I'm afraid I'm not at liberty to reveal that kind of information. Suffice it to say that Miss Kyte—or at any rate, the school—has its enemies.

Miss D'Vere enters

Miss D'Vere Excuse me, I think I left my cigarettes in here. (*To him*) You're still here, I see.

Mr Smith (*collecting his papers together and putting them into his briefcase*) And shall be for quite some time. I'd like now to inspect— the East Wing. It's covered in debris, I gather. (*He moves to the door*)

Miss D'Vere How lucky you didn't come last week—it might have fallen on you.

Mr Smith (*stopping at the door*) Someone might inform Miss Kyte that I shall need to speak to her before I leave. She can't hide away for ever. Oh, by the way—the old well in the grounds—it's not still used by the school, surely?

Miss D'Vere It still has water, I believe—but it isn't used anymore.

Mr Smith (*delving into his briefcase*) I suspect it is. Though not for collecting water. (*He produces a half empty bottle of Gordon's gin and holds it up*) I found this in there. It's still half full. One of your pupils, would you say? Or a member of staff?

He half smiles, turns and exits into the hall

Miss Duke (*furious, about to go after him*) You...!

Miss D'Vere (*knowing her temper*) Miss Duke! Language!

Miss Duke I could cut his ——

Miss D'Vere Yes, I'm sure you could, but it's not going to help.

Miss Duke But he's planning to close the school down, D'Vere!

Miss D'Vere Sit down—calm yourself.

Miss Duke But what about *them*? Molly and Kitty, McBain and Rose Pink? Marjorie, for God's sake!

Miss D'Vere What about us?

Miss Duke What do we matter? We're young enough to start again—but them. They're too old. What would become of them? They don't even belong to a union or anything.

Miss D'Vere Nor do we.

Miss Duke They won't receive a penny in compensation—just thrown on the scrap-heap.

Miss D'Vere Kyte will just have to sell the place and give them some money.

Miss Duke Oh, you can just see that happening, can't you? This is her home, remember. And their home as well. What kind of a life do any of them have away from here?

Miss D'Vere I need a cigarette. (*She looks about for them*)

Miss Duke We can't just sit here, D'Vere—we've got to do something. If only we knew who the hell had complained.

Miss D'Vere (*still looking*) One of the parents, obviously.

Miss Duke It couldn't have been. It must have come from someone here.

Miss D'Vere How do you make that out?

Miss Duke He knew about the ceiling in the East Wing. None of the parents know about that yet.

Miss Fisher enters, distressed

Miss Fisher This is shocking—Bickerstaff tells us that dreadful man wants to close the school.

Miss Duke (*rising*) Hang on—I'm getting the others.

Miss D'Vere What're you doing now?

Miss Duke (*moving to the exit*) Where's that bell?

Miss Duke exits

Miss Fisher (*bewildered, sitting in her chair*) What are we going to do, D'Vere?

We hear the handbell ringing out in the hall

Miss D'Vere I don't know, Molly.

Miss Fisher Does all this mean we're going to lose our jobs?

Miss D'Vere (*trying to comfort her*) If there isn't a school, there won't be any jobs, lovey.

Miss Fisher I can't afford to stop working. I can't stay at home with Doris and Joan waiting to die, can I?

Miss Duke enters, with the bell in hand

Miss Duke That'll fetch them. All right, Molly?

Miss Fisher And what about a pension? Will we get a pension? Joan got a good pension from the Civil Service.

Miss McBain and Miss Kershaw enter quickly

Miss Kershaw What was the bell for?

Miss Duke I need you all in here.

Miss McBain Rose Pink's in a dreadful state. She seems to think we all suspect her of reporting us.

Miss Kershaw (*taking up a judo stance*) Where is that odious little man— shall I give him the chop?

Miss Duke Just sit down, Kitty. We need to talk.

Miss Pink enters, close to tears. She is followed by Miss Bickerstaff

Miss Bickerstaff I did nothing of the kind, Miss Pink. (*To the rest of them*) Take no notice of this woman—she's raving.

Miss Pink (*in a state*) Yes, you did, and you can't deny it. In fact, I have a witness. Miss D'Vere, you were present when she said it.

Miss D'Vere Was I—what, Rose?

Miss Pink (*pointing at Miss Bickerstaff*) This woman—our so-called Deputy Head—accused me of sneaking to the authorities. Did you or did you not hear her?

Miss D'Vere No, dear, that's not what happened at all. You threatened to write to the authorities, Rose.

Everyone talks at once

Miss Fisher So, it was Pink!

Miss Kershaw I don't believe it!
Miss McBain Typical of a musician—to fiddle while Rome is burning!
Miss D'Vere That's what happened, Rose. She didn't accuse you!
Miss Duke (*ringing the bell and shouting*) Quiet! Please!

Silence. They all look across at Miss Duke

We shall get nowhere if we all talk at once. Now, please, ladies—take a seat.

They all sit in their own chairs

Good. Now—quite calmly—Miss Pink, did you complain, in writing, about our school?
Miss Pink I most certainly did not.
Miss Duke Did you do anything at all that might have caused that man to come here?
Miss Pink No. God's honour. On my twin sister Candy's life!

Miss McBain bursts out laughing

Why is that woman laughing?
Miss McBain (*laughing*) Rose and Candy Pink—don't you think that's funny?
Miss Fisher (*sternly*) McBain—pull yourself together.
Miss McBain (*stopping at once*) Sorry, Molly. (*To the others*) Do forgive me. I think I'm becoming hysterical.
Miss Duke Look, ladies—we have a crisis on our hands. I'm afraid it very much looks as if someone—and by that I mean someone here—has betrayed us.

Silence. They all look at each other

Miss Bickerstaff But that's nonsense. No-one here would do such a dreadful thing. (*She pauses*) Surely…

Mrs Godfrey appears at the door. They all turn to look at her

Mrs Godfrey Nobody's even touched their sardines. Here, what you all looking at me for?

Miss Duke Come in, Vi.

Mrs Godfrey comes into the room

Sit down.

Mrs Godfrey sheepishly sits

Now, Vi, we want the absolute truth. Have you been writing nasty letters?

Mrs Godfrey No, miss. Why would I do that?

Miss D'Vere gets on her knees and looks under the sofa

Miss Duke (*irritated*) D'Vere—what the hell are you doing now?

Miss D'Vere My cigarettes—nobody's seen them, have they?

Miss McBain (*suddenly*) What about the Head?

Miss Bickerstaff What about her?

Miss McBain Oughtn't she to be told? About all this?

Miss Bickerstaff She's locked up in her room. Dressed in black by now, I shouldn't wonder.

Miss D'Vere sits on the sofa, leaning on a cushion

Mrs Godfrey No, she ain't, miss. She's gorn fishing.

Miss Bickerstaff Fishing. Vi, please don't tell lies.

Mrs Godfrey Honest to God, miss. The last I saw of her, she was poking down the old well with a long pole and a meat hook.

Miss D'Vere looks behind the cushion of the sofa she has been leaning on

Barmy. In the head. Like old Finch.

Miss D'Vere Oh, my God!

Miss Duke What is it?

From behind the cushion, Miss D'Vere produces a partly knitted cardigan still on its needles

Miss D'Vere Look what I've found—Marjorie Cross's knitting.

Miss Duke What about her bag?

Miss D'Vere No bag, I'm afraid—but there is this.

She now produces an empty half bottle of Gordon's gin. She holds it up for all to see

Miss Duke Not another bottle of... Oh, poor Marjorie.

Miss McBain What is going on here? What does all this mean?

Miss Kyte appears at the french windows. She holds aloft a large canvas knitting bag which is still dripping with water

Miss Kyte That is precisely what I should like to know, Miss McBain.

They all turn to Miss Kyte

The mystery is solved. This disgusting bag was at the bottom of my well.

Miss D'Vere Marjorie Cross's knitting bag!

Miss Kyte And if anyone would care to look inside, they will find my little Trixie—stone dead!

She drops the bag to the floor—it lands with a dull, death-like thud. The ladies recoil in horror and look away

Miss Cross appears in the doorway from the hall

Miss Cross (*enquiringly, bird-like*) Did someone ring the bell?

The Lights begin to fade as the others all look at her. The girls' choir is heard singing "What a Friend We Have in Jesus"

The Lights slowly fade to Black-out

CURTAIN

ACT II

It is evening. Outside in the garden it is already starting to get dark

A clock strikes eight

The Lights slowly come up on the staffroom. The various lamps that spread light and shade in equal amounts give the room an air of melancholy

On the table, ominously placed, sit Mr Smith's briefcase and umbrella

Miss Kyte, now dressed in various shades of mourning, is lying, feet up, on the sofa, her eyes closed, but not asleep, a hand to her brow. Miss Cross is in her chair, knitting quietly on her new grey cardigan. Miss McBain, in her chair, is reading Miss D'Vere's copy of Wuthering Heights, *still dressed in her white coat. Miss Kershaw is lying on the floor downstage, quietly lifting each leg in turn by way of exercise. Miss Fisher, still in her academic gown, is fast asleep in her chair*

The clock stops striking. Silence

Miss Kyte (*after a moment, not moving, with anguish in her voice*) What time was that?
Miss McBain (*engrossed in her book*) Eight o'clock.
Miss Kyte (*to herself*) Oh, God.

Pause

Miss Pink enters quietly from the hall. She has a brown cardigan about her shoulders, her purse in her hand

Miss Pink (*although she knows no-one is interested*) I've just made my call to Agnes Finch.

There is no reply. She sits in her chair

I do so every evening at about this time. (*She puts on glasses and settles down with a copy of* Music and Musicians)

Miss Kyte (*with her eyes closed*) I hope you put the money in the little box.

Miss Pink I never use the telephone in the office. Never. I always walk to the call box in the lane. (*She pauses*) Miss Finch sends her regards to everyone and hopes to be back by November. (*She waits for a response, then reads her magazine in silence*)

Miss Kyte We'd better hide the matches. Just in case.

Pause

Is there a chill? I feel a chill.

Miss Kershaw (*still exercising*) I could close the windows. Might get a bit stuffy though.

After a moment, Miss McBain shuts her book with a snap and sighs. Miss Kyte flinches at the sound

Miss McBain It's remarkable, you know. Those sisters' lives must have been dull in the extreme and yet they could write with such passion.

Miss Kershaw Sisters?

Miss McBain The Brontës.

Miss Kershaw Oh, them. The Dreary Dollies.

Miss Pink gives her a look

Miss McBain I once took my mother to Haworth. Quite recently in fact. Her only concern was how much it must cost to heat the place. (*She pauses*) Shall we be playing bridge this evening?

Miss Kershaw Couldn't concentrate, dear—could you?

Miss McBain (*with her head back, eyes closed*) Perhaps not.

Miss Pink (*after a pause, taking off her glasses*) I've always thought it quite pleasant—sitting here in the afterglow of an autumn afternoon. If ever I do have to leave here—this is the time of day I shall miss the most. (*She pulls a hanky from her sleeve, and wipes her nose*) I had hoped to do *Chu Chin Chow* next term.

Miss Kyte Have you been drinking, Pink?

Miss Cross looks up shyly at the mention of drink

Miss Duke and Miss D'Vere enter from the garden, dressed in cardigans and wellingtons. Miss Duke carries a spade

(*Sensing their presence*) Is it done?

Miss D'Vere Yes. Miss Duke dug the hole. Mrs Godfrey and I——

Miss Kyte (*raising a hand in protest*) Don't! Spare me the details, please. Where is she now?

Miss D'Vere She's gone to make the cocoa.

Miss Duke and Miss D'Vere change into shoes

Miss Kyte The dog, Miss D'Vere, the dog. Where is she lain?

Miss D'Vere We've made a cross of stones—you can't miss it.

Miss Kyte She'll be with Mother now.

The others look at each other. Silence. Miss D'Vere sits at the table. During the following, she idly looks through the unposted letters which still lie there

Miss Cross (*consumed with guilt; suddenly*) I'm so sorry—so very, very sorry.

Miss Duke (*sincerely, sitting in her chair*) Don't worry about it, Marjorie.

Miss Cross (*flushed, shiny*) No, it must be said—I'm ashamed to my finger tips. It's a disgusting habit, I know—but I can't help it, you see.

Miss D'Vere (*gently*) We understand, dear. It's not important now.

Miss Cross Oh, but it is. It's an affliction, do you see—an illness. I've always been terribly nervous of everything—highly strung, my mother called it. But it helped me to overcome all that. I could stop, if I wanted, I'm sure I could, but I get so tired all the time. Upset by the slightest thing. That's when I find I need it. I know you understand, Miss D'Vere, because you have your cigarettes. We all need something, don't we? But I never had it in my classroom—never. Or in my little bedroom. I thought it was safe hidden out there down the well—or in my knitting bag. But I didn't kill your little dog, Miss Kyte. I could never do a thing like that. I do hope you believe that.

Miss Kyte (*unmoved*) Until the culprit is found, Miss Cross, I can believe nothing.

Miss Cross (*quietly*) I see. (*She lowers her head*)

Miss Bickerstaff enters, looking tired and worn, but still efficient with a large address book in her hand

Miss Bickerstaff Well, I've phoned as many parents as I could. They, very kindly, will telephone others and pass the word along. I'm afraid one of us will have to be at the station tomorrow, just in case.

They all look at her   Miss Kyle rolls her eyes

Well, what else can I do? It's no good them arriving here and having to turn them all away again.

Miss Kyte (*fully awake now*) What did you tell them?

Miss Bickerstaff I couldn't tell them the truth, could I? Not yet, anyway.

Miss Kyte So?

Miss Bickerstaff I said that due to an unfortunate set of circumstances the start of term would be delayed for two days.

Miss McBain Two days. And what will you tell them after two days?

Miss Bickerstaff If you think you can do any better, Miss McBain, I suggest you do so.

Miss Kershaw (*getting up from the floor*) All right, Dorothy, keep calm, dear. We're all trying to think of something.

Miss Bickerstaff I see no signs of it. Everything is being left to me as usual. (*She sits*)

Pause
Sudden sit upright.

Miss Kyte It's a black day for Kyte's.

Miss Bickerstaff It's not exactly a red-letter day for any of us, Ursula.

Miss Kyte Headmistress, if you please. You know I never allow intimacy in school time.

Miss Bickerstaff (*her nerve beginning to crack*) But it isn't school time, is it? We're not even a school anymore. We're nothing. A collection of displaced women in a broken-down, almost derelict Gothic mansion, soon to be abandoned if that man has his way. And we sit here and do nothing—just allow him to walk in and trample all over us.

Miss Kyte He was sent by the Queen, Bickerstaff.

Miss Bickerstaff Please don't talk rubbish, Headmistress.

Miss Kyte He's a government inspector, Dorothy—he has the power to do anything he likes.

Miss Bickerstaff Where is he now—still prowling around?

Miss McBain He's in the loft above the East Wing. He came asking for a flashlight, left his briefcase and umbrella, and disappeared again.

Miss Kershaw That was at least an hour ago.

Miss Bickerstaff (*on the edge, rising*) I cannot stand all this awful tension.

Miss Kershaw Relax, Dorothy. Cocoa will soon be here.

Miss Bickerstaff Cocoa? Cocoa? Some of Marjorie's gin would do us all
more good! (*She pauses*) I'm sorry, Marjorie.

Miss Kershaw A good old sprint round the playing field, that's what we
all need—instead of sitting here moping. Anybody game?

No response

Oh, well, any news—let me know.

Miss Kershaw jogs off through the french windows

Miss Pink (*rising*) I think I'll go to my room, if no-one minds. At least
we can stay put for tonight—no?

No reply

Miss Pink exits into the hall

Miss Kyte Is Miss Fisher still with us?

Miss McBain (*shaking Miss Fisher*) Molly? Molly, dear?

Miss Fisher (*waking with a start*) Erm? What is it—time for lessons?

Miss McBain No, dear. No more lessons, I'm afraid.

Miss Fisher (*realizing where she is*) Oh, God—is it all true, then?

Miss McBain I fear so, Molly.

Miss Fisher (*turning on Miss Kyte*) This is all her fault!

Miss McBain Don't, dear—leave it now.

Miss Fisher She couldn't care less about us. Her mother would never
have seen us in this mess. What's left for me, Ursula Kyte? Tell me that!
Doris in a stroke—Joan with her grand ideas—me tearing around—
waiting on them hand and foot. (*She is near to tears*) I'd rather be dead!

Miss McBain (*kneeling in front of her*) There, there, don't worry.
Something will turn up.

Miss Fisher (*weeping*) I've been here all my life, Phoebe, all my life. I
looked forward to ending my days here. Then someone could do to me
what they did to that wretched dog of hers.

Miss Bickerstaff (*compassionately*) No-one's going to chloroform you,
Molly. Try to look on the bright side, dear.

Miss Fisher (*rising, her anger unleashed*) You've a lot to answer for,
    Ursula Kyte!
Miss Kyte (*quietly*) Take her away, please, Miss McBain.
Miss Fisher That's what you'd like, isn't it? For the lot of us just to be
    carted off.
Miss McBain (*trying to lead her away*) Come along, Molly. Please don't
    distress yourself.
Miss Fisher (*shrugging her off*) I can stand alone, McBain, thank you—
    I don't need to be supported. (*She tries to get at Miss Kyte*)

Miss McBain restrains her

    You even saw poor old Agnes Finch carted away to the madhouse. I
    wouldn't be surprised if you started those fires yourself—you wicked,
    dried-up old bitch! (*She attempts to strike out at Miss Kyte*)
Miss D'Vere (*jumping up*) That's enough now, Molly. Come on—let's
    get you out of here.

Miss D'Vere and Miss McBain escort Miss Fisher away

Miss Fisher (*weeping*) I'm so sorry. I'm so dreadfully sorry.

    They exit into the hall

*There is a dreadful silence. Miss Kyte looks pale, shaken. For the first time
we see her vulnerability even though she does her best to look dignified*

Miss Bickerstaff (*quietly, embarrassed*) I'd better see if there's anything
    I can do.

    She exits into the hall

Miss Cross quietly collects her knitting, rises, and moves to the door

Miss Cross Excuse me. I'll just… Yes.

    She escapes out into the hall

Silence

Miss Duke (*at length, sincerely*) I'm sorry.

Miss Kyte (*quietly, staring into space*) There's no need to feel sorry. The moment was long overdue.

Miss Duke Would you like me to leave?

Miss Kyte You must do as you wish.

Pause

My mother was quite a remarkable woman, Miss Duke. In many ways, I wish you had known her. (*She pauses*) It was a habit of hers... Collecting misfits—eccentrics—spinster teachers whose short-comings had failed to gain them employment elsewhere. (*She pauses*) She is sorely missed. As I'm sure you must have gathered by now. (*She pauses*) I hated her, Miss Duke. Does that surprise you?

Pause

She knew just how much I detested this place—how unsuitable I was to become a teacher. And yet, even on her deathbed, she made me promise to continue running the school. Perhaps she wanted to punish me in some way—knowing what an unholy mess I was bound to make of the job. Her real concern, of course, was for the staff. She wanted me to take care of them—to love them as she herself had loved them. (*She pauses*) But I'm incapable of doing that, Miss Duke.

Miss Duke (*after a pause*) Why are you telling me all this?

Miss Kyte (*smiling*) I can't imagine. How strange. Perhaps I feel safe with you. You're the only member of staff I've taken on under my regime. (*She looks at her for the first time*) Was I careless? Did I break the mould? Perhaps you don't really belong here.

Miss Duke But I do. I'm perfectly happy here.

Miss Kyte Don't be deceived. Therein lies the trap.

Miss Duke Not all of these people are misfits, Miss Kyte. Not all of them are as unhappy as you appear to be.

Miss Kyte Oh, come now. Miss Cross? Miss Pink? Dorothy Bickerstaff?

Miss Duke Miss Bickerstaff adores her life here. Surely you can see that. And Miss McBain—she seems perfectly straightforward.

Miss Kyte Phoebe McBain tells lies. Her aged mother in Edinburgh? She doesn't exist. She died many years ago. Miss McBain, like the rest of them, lives her life with the cuckoos.

Miss Duke (*disturbed*) And Miss Kershaw?

Miss Kyte I do not intend to give you a catalogue of the sins and omissions of my staff, Miss Duke.

Miss Duke My friend then. Miss D'Vere. What about her? *Move to Duke*

Miss Kyte Miss D'Vere has been more fortunate than the others. You came along. Don't leave her here to rot with the rest of us.

Mr Smith enters quietly from the hall. He looks dusty and carries a flashlight
Move away from Duke towards Smith into space

Miss Kyte (*sarcastically*) Ah, the stranger. And carrying a torch for one of us already.

Mr Smith (*putting the torch on the table*) May I return this—thank you.

Miss Kyte Have you discovered anything more untoward on your journey through my school?

Mr Smith In the words of Alice, Miss Kyte—it gets curiouser and curiouser.

Miss Kyte Really. Do tell us.

Mr Smith Half-consumed bottles of gin in a disused well. A murdered dog in the same place.

Miss Kyte You'll be able to tell your grandchildren.

Mr Smith And now the ceiling in the East Wing. I'm sorry to report that it didn't fall down of its own accord. It was pushed. Several large holes have been made in the loft above that ceiling, thus causing it to cave in when it did.

Miss Kyte How intriguing, Miss Duke. The man's a regular Hercule Poirot.

Mr Smith There are also dead rats in your cellar.

Miss Kyte (*rising to her full height, a hand at her throat*) I must go and pay my last respects to my dog. I'll be there if I'm needed. (*She moves to the windows*)

Mr Smith (*trying to detain her*) We must talk, Miss Kyte—soon.

Miss Kyte I have nothing to say. Good-evening.

Miss Kyte exits through the french windows

Mr Smith She seems—unusual—Miss Kyte.

Miss Duke She is unusual, Mr Smith. But then, so are most of us here at Kyte's.

He just smiles at her

Tell me—when you arrived—you already knew about the ceiling?
Mr Smith I did.
Miss Duke May I ask who told you?
Mr Smith No-one actually told us, Miss Duke. That piece of information was contained in one of the letters of complaint.
Miss Duke One of the letters. There were more?
Mr Smith There were two. One typed and anonymous, the other handwritten and signed.
Miss Duke (*hoping to catch him out*) By whom?

He just smiles again

Have you much more to do before you wipe us from the face of the earth?
Mr Smith Not a lot. I still have to look through the school records—lists of past examination results—that kind of thing.
Miss Duke You'll find them impeccable. Our standards of achievement here have always been outstanding.
Mr Smith Good. I do hope so. Can you tell me where such records are kept?
Miss Duke In the office of Dorothy Bickerstaff. She keeps them most meticulously.
Mr Smith Thank you. (*He turns to go*)
Miss Duke Tell me, do you receive a reward for this kind of work, a bonus, a knighthood?

He knows she is trying to insult him but has learned never to rise to the bait

  He exits into the hall

Left alone, Miss Duke seems both distressed and annoyed. A thought strikes her. She goes to the table and looks at the two letters she left there earlier. She picks up one of the letters, thinks about it, and is about to tear it up

  Miss D'Vere enters quietly

Miss D'Vere All right?
Miss Duke (*startled, turning*) Oh, God! (*She hides the letter behind her back*) Don't do that, D'Vere.

Miss D'Vere (*laughing*) I'm sorry. I saw him leave—I thought… (*She pauses*) You look flustered—that's not like you.

Miss Duke (*knowing she's been caught, showing the letter*) It's just this. I've changed my mind.

Miss D'Vere (*lighting a cigarette, sitting*) Oh. I see.

Miss Duke Do you want to see it?

Miss D'Vere Why on earth should I want to see it? It's only a letter to the nice people at the hotel. Isn't it?

Miss Duke No. Not this one. It's addressed to Mr Maurice Newbury. (*She pauses*) I'm sorry, D'Vere.

Miss D'Vere Don't worry. I'm sorry too. I saw the letter earlier. When I was sitting at the table.

Miss Duke You!

Miss D'Vere Careful—remember where we are.

Miss Duke Why didn't you say anything?

Miss D'Vere There hasn't exactly been time, has there?

Miss Duke tears the letter in half

D'Vere Why do that?

Miss Duke I told you. I've changed my mind.

Miss D'Vere He offered you a job. I know all about it. He told me—the morning you were late down to breakfast.

Miss D'Vere He's a nice man, D'Vere. Really.

Miss Duke I'm sure. And a very high-powered one. Chief Education Officer for where? Where all the action is, I'll be bound. And he's unmarried. Good looking.

Miss Duke It seemed like a good opportunity, that's all. More money— promotion. A chance to get away from here.

Miss D'Vere looks hurt

I'm sorry. That came out sounding all wrong.

No reply

You know nothing about me, do you? I have a past, you know. I came here to start afresh. I invented a different me. That's easy to do out here.

Miss D'Vere Does Miss Kyte know your history?

Miss Duke I'm not sure. She's never said.

Pause

Miss D'Vere When will you go?

Miss Duke Go?

Miss D'Vere Will you take the Green Line or will the dashing Mr Newbury fetch you in his restored Lagonda?

Miss Duke I'm not going. (*She realizes the error*) Oh, I see… You thought… No, I'd written to tell him I wasn't interested in his job. That's why I tore it up—I'm even less interested now.

Miss D'Vere But why? You need a job more than ever.

Miss Duke Something will turn up. (*She smiles*) We can look for a job together, can't we?

Miss D'Vere is relieved. She smiles

Mrs Godfrey enters, with her trolley loaded with mugs and cocoa in a jug

Mrs Godfrey Cocoa up! Shall I ring the bell?

Miss D'Vere You'd better. It may even be our last mug of cocoa at Kyte's.

Mrs Godfrey Shouldn't be surprised. Still—that's life, as my old man's forever saying!

She exits into the hall

Miss Duke At least Vi seems cheerful about all this.

The handbell is heard ringing

Mrs Godfrey (*off; shouting*) Cocoa, come an' get it, you lot!

Miss Kershaw sprints in from the garden

Miss Kershaw Cocoa time, girls. Things can't be too bad if there's cocoa. (*She pours her own cocoa*)

Mrs Godfrey enters

Mrs Godfrey There ain't no biscuits, ladies, so you'll have to whistle for them!

Miss Kershaw No food arrived yet, Vi?

Mrs Godfrey (*sitting, exhausted*) No. And it won't now, will it?

Miss Kershaw Why on earth not?

Mrs Godfrey Been on the phone, ain't I? "Where's my soddin' supplies?" I said to him—and you know what that saucy sod said? (*She lowers her voice*) She ain't paid the bill from last term, has she?

Miss D'Vere Who—Old Kyte—Hawk?

Mrs Godfrey Nah—her. Old Bicker-knickers! She's losing her grip, ask me. End up with old Finchy in the nut-house, she will.

Miss Pink enters

The ladies all help themselves to the cocoa, then take up their usual seats

Miss Pink Another bell?

Miss Kershaw Cocoa, Rose. Get it while it's hot, dear.

Miss Duke (*drinking*) It isn't.

Miss Pink (*pouring her own cocoa*) I thought there'd been another crisis.

Miss Kershaw (*sitting*) We don't need another, Rose. We've still got the old one.

Miss Pink We still don't know who killed little Trixie, then?

Mrs Godfrey She definitely thinks that was me.

Miss D'Vere Nonsense, Vi. You're becoming paranoid.

Mrs Godfrey I tell you she does, miss. You can see it in her eyes—she won't look at me.

Miss Duke Don't worry, Vi. We know it wasn't you.

Miss D'Vere (*puzzled*) Do we?

Miss McBain enters

Miss McBain Molly's feeling much better. Regretting all she said, of course. Ah, cocoa. (*She helps herself to the cocoa*)

Miss Duke (*deep in thought*) Phoebe—if I needed some chloroform would you have it?

Miss McBain Yes. In my lab. What in the world do you need chloroform for?

Miss D'Vere What are you up to?

Miss Duke I'm not up to anything.

Miss Kyte enters from the garden

Everyone goes quiet—not used to seeing her down here in the evenings.
Miss Duke has an eye on Miss Kyte throughout the following exchanges

Miss Kyte Most tastefully executed, Miss Duke, Miss D'Vere. I like
where you've placed her. Under the oak. Very peaceful.
Mrs Godfrey (*two-faced*) Would you like some nice hot cocoa, madam?
Miss Kyte Thank you, Godfrey—I think perhaps I will.
Mrs Godfrey (*pouring cocoa*) Shall you have it in your room as usual,
madam? I don't mind popping up with it, I'm sure.
Miss Kyte No, no. I'll have it here. With my friends. (*She sits*)

The others look at each other—they've never been called friends before

Mrs Godfrey (*giving Miss Kyte the cocoa*) There we are. Warm your little
cockles will that—after the day you've had, eh? (*She goes back to her
trolley*) Poor cow!

Miss Kyte sips her cocoa

Miss Kyte How calming are the effects of cocoa and close colleagues.
Thank you.
Mrs Godfrey Well, I'd best just slip into my kitchen perhaps for the very
last time. (*She gets out a tea towel from her apron*) Give my surfaces a
final wipe—turn the gas off—turn out the light. Sorry—I'm filling up.
(*She blows her nose on the tea towel*)

She rushes out in tears

Miss Kyte Dear Mrs Godfrey. Whatever her faults, like us all, she's
remained loyal to Kyte's. I heard the bell. Does that mean everyone will
be down for cocoa?
Miss McBain All except Miss Cross—she usually does without.
Miss Kyte Good. I want to talk to you all.

Miss Fisher enters quietly, head bowed in shame

Miss Kershaw Ah, Molly. Don't look so glum, dear.

Miss Fisher (*going straight to Miss Kyte*) That was unforgivable of me, Ursula. Quite, quite unforgivable. I can't think what came over me, but I had no right at all to say those dreadful things to you.

Miss Kershaw and Miss Pink look puzzled, having missed the row earlier

This whole wretched business has come as such a shock to me. To us all. Am I forgiven, dear?

Miss Kershaw rises and begins pouring cocoa for Miss Fisher

Miss Kyte Don't be silly, Molly. (*She rises and takes Miss Fisher to her breast*) Of course you're forgiven. Just forget it ever happened.

Miss Pink (*puzzled*) Have I missed something?

Miss D'Vere Nothing important, Rose.

Miss Fisher (*going to her chair*) I was rude to Miss Kyte, Rose. Abominably rude. (*She sits and takes her cocoa from Miss Kershaw*)

Miss Pink Oh, dear. It seems a day for losing one's temper. Miss McBain, I, too, was very rude to you over our having to share and I would like to apologize.

Miss McBain Don't worry, Rose. I wasn't exactly charm or tact myself. I'm sorry too. I ought not to have laughed at your sister's name.

Miss Pink I can understand why you laughed. It's happened all our lives. Even at school we were laughed at. Candy is actually short for Candida. Rose and Candida Pink. Parents can be so cruel—so thoughtless— burdening their offspring with ludicrous labels.

Silence. All the ladies sip their cocoa. Calm has descended. We can almost feel this odd group of ladies coming ever closer

If we are to disband, if the school ceases to exist, I do hope we don't all lose touch. Candida and I, we have a small house in Sussex—not very far from the sea—and you'd all be more than welcome to visit us.

The others listen, obviously quite touched by her gesture

Afternoon tea perhaps—or an evening meal. Candy loves to cook. (*She pauses*) Miss Kyte, we'd be very honoured if you could join us. And Miss McBain—perhaps you could bring your mother.

Miss McBain That would be very nice, Rose. Thank you.

Miss Cross enters quietly from the hall

The others are surprised to see her

Miss Kershaw Good God—it's Marjorie.

Miss Cross May I? I thought… Just for this evening, I might try a mug of cocoa. Only if there's one to spare.

Miss Kershaw (*rising*) Course there is, lovey. Come in, dear—pull up a pew. (*She pours cocoa for Miss Cross*) Not used to having you with us in the evenings, what? Still, I suppose you got your bedtime drink from the old well, eh?

Miss Fisher Kitty!

Miss Cross It's all right, Miss Fisher—really.

Miss Fisher No, it is not all right!

Miss Kershaw (*handing the cocoa to Miss Cross*) Oh, come off, Molly. Best to face up to things, eh, Marjorie?

Miss Cross (*smiling*) Yes. (*She sips her cocoa*)

Miss Kershaw That's been the trouble with us lot. We've never faced up to things. Now look at the mess we're in. A collection of old pots and no shelf to put us on. Look at me—who'd want me at my age? Useless old fart, qualified for nothing—worthless!

Miss D'Vere You're not at all worthless, Kitty. Or useless.

Miss Kershaw All right—but *they* don't know that, D'Vere. The powers that be—the little man who sits behind his desk and interviews me. "Twenty years at Gwendolen Kyte's," he'll say, "where the hell's that?"

Miss McBain Miss Kyte will give us testimonials, won't you?

Miss Kershaw Testimonials! Come on, Maccers, we may as well leave here with a stick of Blackpool rock. They want youth, dear. Youth, good looks and qualifications!

Miss Fisher I'm afraid she's right. We're past it.

Miss Kershaw Past it, Molly. Some of us never even had it! Look at me— I show off—pretend to be a woman of the world—laugh at dirty jokes I don't even understand—but I often stand in that changing room and listen to our girls discussing what they've been up to with their boyfriends and I blush in ignorance. No, we've got to face it, ladies— it's not the overture they're playing out there—it's the bloody finale! (*She sits depressed*)

Silence. Everyone is depressed now

Miss Pink (*after a pause*) I've got a little money put by. I mean—I could always lend some to anyone if they're in need.

Miss Kershaw You hang on to your money, Rose dear. You're going to need it.

Silence falls again

Miss Duke You're very quiet, Miss Kyte. Have you nothing to say?

Miss Kyte There's no need for any of you to worry about money. Do you think I haven't thought about all that? There's this place for a start—it must be worth a fortune. Even if it is falling apart.

Miss Fisher But where would you live, Ursula?

Miss Kyte As far away from here as possible. I was born here, ladies. Born here, lived here, educated here, conceived here, for heaven's sake. The last thing I want is to be buried here, please.

Miss Duke You're happy to see the school close then?

Miss Kyte Of course I am. You all know very well I am. I'm sick of the place—tired. I need some time for myself.

Miss Fisher We know, Ursula. We know you only kept the school on to please your mother.

Miss Kyte (*rising, moving about the room as she speaks*) No, Molly. Not for my mother. I kept it on for you, dear. You and Agnes Finch—Kitty here—McBain, Miss Cross and Rose Pink. (*She pauses*) And for Dorothy Bickerstaff. You've seen the silly woman—she's in paradise running the place—in ecstasy with her charts, her papers and her interminable lists.

Miss Bickerstaff enters unnoticed

She loves the school—she loves the girls far more than I could ever do. She thinks she's happy—and maybe she is, Miss Duke, but she fails to see that life is passing her by. What is the point of all this, ladies? Why do we do it?

Miss Bickerstaff We do it for the girls, Miss Kyte.

They all turn to look at her

They need us. Rely upon us. We show them the way—shape their destinies.

Only Miss Duke has her eye on Miss Kyte during the following

Miss Kyte What absolute tosh, Dorothy. You're deluded, dear. We act as
child-minders for parents who don't want their offspring at home with
them. And do you think the girls love us? They may, in years to come,
just recall our name at some smart suburban cocktail party. Scoff, poke
fun at us, wonder if we're alive or dead. What do we do for them—tell
me—what? (*To Miss Fisher*) Teach them their sums? (*To Miss D'Vere*)
Pressure them into reading *Wuthering Heights*? They can do that for
themselves, D'Vere. (*To Miss Duke*) Inform them about the varying
currents in the North Sea—that Everest is high—the date of Napoleon's
birthday? Who cares? (*To Miss McBain*) How to cause a minor
explosion—the wonders of litmus paper? Well?

No-one replies

A machine could do all that, ladies. They could sit in front of a television
screen and learn all that without even leaving home! (*She moves to her
seat*) No, that little man upstairs was right—we're outmoded, out of
date, old-fashioned. (*She sits*)

Miss Fisher I never knew you felt like this, Ursula.

Miss Kyte Only because you've never asked me, Molly. Ladies, I beg
you—is it not time to let go? Isn't this the golden opportunity? The place
is falling down about us. What next? A long parade to some cemetery
to bury each other?

Silence. She has had her effect upon them all

Miss Duke (*at length, quietly, not accusingly*) It was you who wrote to
the authorities, Miss Kyte, wasn't it?

Miss Kyte (*resigned to tell only the truth from now on*) Yes. Yes, of course
it was me.

Pause. They all look at her

I typed it on Dorothy's machine. (*She pauses*) I gave Mrs Godfrey's
silly daughter half a crown to deliver it by hand.

Miss Duke And the ceiling in the East Wing—that was your doing too?

Miss Kyte What an achievement that was. Each day during the holidays,
when Dorothy was busy in her office, I was up in the loft. It took a month
and it was a swine—but finally I got the better of it. A week last Monday,
just as we were having tea—it came crashing down.

Everyone is wide-eyed and speechless

Miss Bickerstaff The woman's mad. She's mental. (*To Miss Kyte*) Why
did you do that?

Miss Kyte I thought I'd made it obvious. Where could I find the courage
to shut the school and sack you all? You're my responsibility, a legacy
from my dead mother. I thought that if I rendered the building unsafe—
informed the authorities—they would do the job for me.

Miss Fisher But why say all those nasty things about us? About us being
too old—unqualified?

Miss Kyte I didn't, Molly. All that information must have come from
elsewhere.

The women look at each other

Miss Kershaw Not Agnes Finch, surely?

Miss Pink Agnes would never do that—she's my friend.

Miss D'Vere Then who, for heaven's sake?

Miss Duke We could, of course, soon find out.

Miss McBain How?

Miss Duke There's his briefcase. We could always...

Miss Bickerstaff (*appalled*) Miss Duke! You're not suggesting...?.

Miss Kershaw (*jumping up*) I'll do it and to hell! Maccers, you guard the
door in case the blighter comes back.

Miss McBain moves to the door. Miss Kershaw tries to open the case

Oh, bugger—it's locked!

Miss Cross (*rising; shyly*) I'm awfully good at picking locks, actually.
I've had to do it so often.

Miss Kershaw Good old Crossie. Come on, dear—we'll club together
and buy you a bottle of gin.

*Miss Cross takes a hairpin from her hair and sets about the lock. All the
women rise and watch the operation intently*

Miss Pink Isn't this exciting? Just like Enid Blyton!

The lock springs open

Miss Kershaw The woman's a bloody expert! Well done, dear.

Miss Kyte Well, go on, Kitty—don't shilly-shally—look inside.

Miss Kershaw opens the case and brings out a packet of sandwiches and a flask of tea

Miss Kershaw Well, there's these. (*She holds up a pair of bicycle clips*) And these…
Miss Fisher (*short-sighted*) Handcuffs?
Miss Kershaw Bicycle clips, Molly. Hang on—here's what we're after. (*She pulls out two letters in a file*) One letter—typed—not signed…
Miss Kyte That's the one I wrote.
Miss Duke (*getting impatient*) The other letter, Kitty. Where's the other letter?
Miss Kershaw Keep your vest on—give me a chance. (*She reads from the second letter*) "Dear Sir or madam, I think it is my duty to inform you…" (*She reads in silence, mouthing the words*)
Miss Kyte (*annoyed*) "My duty" to what, Kitty?
Miss Kershaw (*shocked by what she reads*) My God, this is almost libellous, girls—it runs us down something chronic! All untrue, of course. Well, most of it.
Miss McBain (*still by the door; nervously*) Put it back, Kitty—I'm sure I can hear him coming.
Miss Duke The signature, Kitty, the signature.
Miss Kershaw "Yours ever so faithfully… Betty Bowker"! The little toe-rag!

There are various cries of surprise

Miss McBain Do put it back, Kitty, please.

Miss Kershaw puts everything back in the case and locks it

Miss Fisher (*stunned, sitting*) Betty Bowker! I can't believe it. After all I did for that girl!
Miss D'Vere (*puzzled*) What?
Miss Fisher (*vaguely*) Well, I can't think offhand—but I taught her maths, didn't I?

Everyone sits in a state of shock

Miss Pink (*flushed, pink with anger*) The slut!

Miss Kershaw Careful, Rose. No strong language, dear.

Miss D'Vere (*rising to put her mug on the trolley*) All this about letters—it's all very well—but it doesn't tell us who put an end to Trixie.

Miss McBain Or why.

Miss Bickerstaff (*awkwardly*) I'd better go and see what that dreadful man is up to in my office. (*She heads for the door*)

Miss Duke (*rising*) No, Dorothy. We'll find out what he's up to. I think you should stay and explain things to Ursula.

Miss Bickerstaff I'm sorry? Explain?

Miss Duke You slipped up earlier this evening, didn't you, dear?

Miss Bickerstaff (*warily*) Did I?

Miss Duke You mentioned chloroform.

Miss Bickerstaff (*she hangs her head*) Yes.

Miss Duke Come along, you lot—we'll leave these two alone.

Miss Kyte (*speechless*) You don't mean...? You can't mean...?

Miss Duke Out, ladies, please.

Miss Duke exits, followed by Miss D'Vere

Miss McBain (*helping Miss Fisher to the door*) I knew my bottles had been disturbed. Come along, Molly.

Miss Fisher I'm afraid I've missed something—what is going on now?

Miss McBain leads Miss Fisher out into the hall

Miss Kershaw Come on, Marjorie—you can show me how to pick a lock, dear.

Miss Kershaw and Miss Cross exit by the french windows

Miss Pink seems quite content to remain seated. Miss Kyte glares at Miss Bickerstaff

Miss Kyte Miss Pink... If we may, please.

Miss Pink Oh, but I'd love to know what happened.

Miss Kyte Later, Miss Pink, later.

Miss Pink (*rising and moving to the windows*) Oh, dear. I always miss the best bits.

Miss Pink exits into the garden

Silence

Miss Kyte (*after a pause*) Can this be true, Dorothy? If so, it was a foul and despicable act. I am shocked. Deeply and profoundly shocked.

Miss Bickerstaff (*recognizing her act, calmly*) There's no need to be, Ursula. There's no-one here to impress. The animal was old—in pain, unloved. I hope, when my time comes, someone will do the same for me.

Miss Kyte Unloved? How dare you?

Miss Bickerstaff Trixie has had more attention paid to her dead than she's had since Gwendolen passed on. The episode is closed. I just hope you never get another pet. You're not by nature given to caring for them.

Miss Kyte (*rising to the windows, hand to mouth*) But to be cast—down a well!

Miss Bickerstaff (*coldly*) It was dead long before it entered the water. I borrowed a concoction from Miss McBain's cupboards. I tried it on the rats in the cellar—they were comatose in seconds.

Miss Kyte Must we...?

Miss Bickerstaff I simply poured some of the stuff on to a rag and placed it by Trixie's food. No fuss—nothing cruel—she merely sniffed it and was gone.

Miss Kyte Please—no more.

Miss Bickerstaff (*determined to finish*) I needed a receptacle in which to place her—I came in here and found Marjorie Cross's bag. That was foolish of me. I had no wish to incriminate her. Thoughts of Miss Cross led me to think of the well. She's always used the same hiding place— even in your mother's day.

Miss Kyte (*turning to her*) I'm... I'm speechless.

Miss Bickerstaff Now, if that is the end of the matter—I have things to do. (*She walks to the door*)

Miss Kyte (*sternly*) It isn't. You take too much upon yourself, Miss Bickerstaff. I am in charge here.

Miss Bickerstaff Not anymore. You've successfully handed everything over to the bailiff.

Miss Kyte (*raging*) The burden was too great and you know it! I could no longer carry it alone.

Miss Bickerstaff (*wounded*) Alone?

Miss Kyte (*sitting on the sofa; calming herself*) All right—so I had you. But surely you must see. I can't sit here till I'm ninety with this millstone around my neck. At least my mother had me—who do I pass it on to?

Miss Bickerstaff I had hoped... I'd always assumed...

Miss Kyte That I'd leave it all to you? Is that what you mean? Good God! And you think I'd tell you even if I had? You're power-crazy, Dorothy. Phoebe McBain's chloroform would have been on double overtime!

Miss Bickerstaff (*taking offence*) I see... (*She marches to the doors*)

Miss Kyte Oh, come back here, you silly woman. It was a joke, dear, a joke.

Miss Bickerstaff I can take a joke as well as the next, but...

Miss Kyte Oh, Dorothy Bickerstaff, may God forgive you. You must be the most humourless woman since Joan of Arc. Why else do you think we're in this mess?

Miss Bickerstaff So I'm to blame for all this?

Miss Kyte Partly—yes. We both are. Oh, do sit down, dear. I hate it when you hover.

Miss Bickerstaff I have things to do, Ursula——

Miss Kyte (*loudly*) Sit down! For once in your life do as you're told, woman!

Silence. Miss Bickerstaff sits in an armchair

I'm not blind, Dorothy. I see how hard you work. I've always known that without you this place would grind to a halt. As to why you do it for the money I pay you—well, I have to admit that is beyond me.

Miss Bickerstaff opens her mouth to speak

Let me finish, please. I admire you, Dorothy, and I shall always be—grateful to you—but why, after all these years, are we still a million miles apart? We could have been friends, talked things over, conversed in the evenings over a glass of sherry, laughed a little at our misfortunes—behaved like normal people, for heaven's sake. We've lived like strangers in this draughty mausoleum.

Miss Bickerstaff just listens, staring out into space

Do you realize I know nothing about you? What you think—what you feel. I don't even know the date of your birthday. And so today—when I discover that you've murdered my dog, what am I to think? Have I been harbouring a monster all these years?

Miss Bickerstaff (*quieter now, warmer*) I simply put your dog to sleep. Any vet would have done the same years ago. I hid it in the well only to spare your feelings. (*She looks at her hands, head bent*) And you know nothing about me because there's nothing to know. Nothing of any importance anyway. You know how I live. You know everything I do. I never leave here. As to friendship—making friends has never been easy for me.

Miss Kyte But I need your friendship now, Dorothy. I need you to tell me that what I've done was right.

Miss Bickerstaff It wasn't, Ursula. What you did was wrong. These people need you. I need you. We need to be wanted—useful to someone—in God's name, what else have we?

Miss Kyte But it's too late. You heard the man from the ministry.

Miss Bickerstaff To hell with the man from the ministry! What does he or any of his colleagues know, anyway?

Miss Kyte But he's in your office now. Searching for even more evidence with which to hang us.

Miss Bickerstaff So what? He won't find anything, Ursula. We have nothing to hide and certainly nothing to be ashamed of.

Miss Kyte We haven't?

Miss Bickerstaff You really know nothing about this school, do you? Everything here is done to the highest standards, Ursula. Standards set by your mother. We can be proud of our achievements.

Miss Kyte But things have moved on, Dorothy—the world's a different place now.

Miss Bickerstaff What of it? Why should that worry us? We play no part in it, anyway. We're here—safe—hidden away—doing what we do best—teaching children and making a bloody good job of it!

Miss Kyte (*warily*) You're becoming heated, Dorothy—I don't like it.

Miss Bickerstaff, impassioned now, moves over and sits beside Miss Kyte and takes hold of her by the shoulders

Miss Bickerstaff Please, Ursula, listen to me. We may be old-fashioned—we may be behind the times—but that is how we choose to be—and what is wrong with it? And the parents—what about them? They must be happy with the school as it is—why else would they keep sending their girls here?

Miss Kyte But the house—it's falling apart. You heard the man—we're overcrowded—the place is becoming unsafe.

Miss Bickerstaff (*enthusiastically*) So? We spend money on it, Ursula. Renovate it, enlarge it, bring it up to scratch.

Miss Kyte But how?

Miss Bickerstaff We do what other schools do, Ursula—ask for money. Beg for it, if necessary. Most of our parents are comfortably off—very wealthy some of them—I'm sure they'd be glad to help. Just think—with a few thousand pounds we could replace the ceiling in the East Wing—build some new classrooms—bring our fire precautions up to date... Who knows—we might even take on more pupils.

Miss Kyte You seem to have thought this out already.

Miss Bickerstaff It's been my dream, Ursula. I could organize it. A fund-raising scheme. Jumble sales, fêtes out on the lawns twice a year—a lottery.

Miss Kyte Jumbles sales, Dorothy. Fêtes? A lottery? Here at Kyte's?

Miss Bickerstaff Why not?

Miss Kyte My staff would never agree to it.

Miss Bickerstaff Ursula—why do you always underestimate them? They want to keep this school open as much as I do. All right, that man out there may think them old-fashioned—a bit odd, a touch eccentric—but they are good teachers—splendid teachers. Caring, dedicated, committed—what more could you want?

Miss Kyte rises slowly and moves downstage. A glimmer of light is beginning to show in her eyes as she stares straight ahead

As I said earlier—they need you now. You can't just drop them—desert them—cast them aside. You've got to fight, Ursula.

Miss Kyte But how, Dorothy, how? I'm not made like my mother. I'm not able to fight.

Miss Bickerstaff You needn't do it alone. We'll help.

As she speaks each name, the others appear from where they went off and group around Miss Bickerstaff on the sofa

Molly and Phoebe... Kitty and Marjorie. Rose Pink... Duke and D'Vere... They'll all help.

Mrs Godfrey runs in from the hall

Mrs Godfrey And me, miss, don't forget me.

Mrs Godfrey's voice causes Miss Kyte to turn and see them all

Miss Kyte Ladies, shame on you—you've all been listening. Please, please sit down.

They all sit in their various seats

You heard all that, I've no doubt.
All We did, Headmistress.
Miss Kyte I'm sorry I did what I did, ladies.
Miss Fisher It wasn't all you, Ursula. Betty Bowker played her part as well.
Miss Kyte What do you say then? We give it a go? We drag our school screaming into the Sixties?

Various cries of "You bet!", "Of course!", "Can't wait!" "We do!", etc.

And the man—how do we deal with him?
Mrs Godfrey We could knock him off. Shove him down the well. No?
Miss Kyte (*sternly*) Godfrey—please!
Miss Bickerstaff We tell him to go. Send him away with a flea in his ear. Tell him we're perfectly aware of our inadequacies and intend to do something about it—right, ladies?
The Others Right!
Miss Kyte Ladies, ladies—what can I say? Mother would have been so proud of you all.
Miss Fisher And you, Ursula. She'd have been proud of you.
Miss Kyte That's it then. We start afresh. The scene is set, ladies. The curtain is about to rise just at the moment we all expected it to fall.

The clock in the hall begins to strike nine

Listen…

On the first stroke of nine, Mr Smith appears in the doorway from the hall, looking smug and self-satisfied

The women all turn to look at him—then slowly rise to their feet. His face changes—he knows he's lost this battle. The Lights begin to fade slowly as the clock continues to chime its way to nine

The Curtain *falls*

FURNITURE AND PROPERTY LIST

Further dressing may be added at the director's discretion

ACT I

On stage: Old leather armchairs
Old horse-hair sofa. *On it:* cushions, copy of *Wuthering Heights*
Large table. *On it:* newspapers, magazines, exercise books
Coloured memos
Miss D'Vere's bag. *In it:* purse with coins
Partly knitted cardigan
Empty half bottle of Gordon's gin

Off stage: Briefcase. *In it:* note-pad, clipboard, pen, papers, half-empty bottle of Gordon's gin, packet of sandwiches, tea flask, file with two letters (**Mr Smith**)
Umbrella (**Mr Smith**)
Ashtray (**Miss D'Vere**)
Old leather suitcase with straps (**Miss McBain**)
Bag (**Miss McBain**)
Gloves (**Miss McBain**)
Exercise books (**Miss Fisher**)
Tea trolley. *On it:* cups, saucers, spoons, tea towel (**Mrs Godfrey**)
Papers and charts (**Miss Bickerstaff**)
2 letters (**Miss Duke**)
MK   Enormous enamel teapot (**Mrs Godfrey**)
Dog's lead (**Miss Kyte**) *Linda*
Handbell (**Mrs Godfrey, Miss Duke**)
Large canvas knitting bag (**Miss Kyte**)

Personal: **Mr Smith:** bicycle clips, watch, business card
Miss D'Vere: cigarettes and lighter
Miss McBain: tweed cape, brown hat, scarf, rubber gloves
Miss Fisher: half glasses (used throughout)
Miss Kershaw: stop watch
Miss Cross: hairpin (used throughout)

ACT II

Set: **Mr Smith**'s briefcase and umbrella
            Miss Duke's and **Miss D'Vere**'s shoes

Strike: Newspapers, magazines, and exercise books from large table
            Miss D'Vere's bag from large table
            Partly knitted cardigan
            Empty half bottle of Gordon's gin
            Half empty bottle of Gordon's gin

Off stage: Knitting (**Miss Cross**)
            Spade (**Miss Duke**)
            Large address book (**Miss Bickerstaff**)
            Flashlight (**Mr Smith**)
            Trolley. *On it:* mugs and jug with cocoa (**Mrs Godfrey**)

Personal: **Mrs Godfrey:** tea-towel

LIGHTING PLOT

Practical fittings required: various lamps
Interior. The same throughout

ACT I

To open: Autumn sunshine effect, slowly increasing

Cue 1	**Miss Kyte** exits *Fade to black-out*	(Page 25)
Cue 2	**Mr Smith** lays his papers before him *Bring up early evening twilight effect*	(Page 25)
Cue 3	**Miss Cross**: "Did someone ring the bell?" *Fade slowly to black-out*	(Page 35)

ACT II

To open: Twilight effect

Cue 4	A clock strikes eight *Slowly turn up lamp lights*	(Page 36)
Cue 5	The women slowly rise to their feet *Fade lights slowly*	(Page 60)

EFFECTS PLOT

ACT I

Cue 1   To open   (Page 1)
           Girls' choir singing "For All the Saints"; fade when ready

Cue 2   **Mr Smith** writes on his clipboard   (Page 1)
           Clock strikes three

Cue 3   **Miss Cross** exits into the garden   (Page 16)
           Hand bell ringing very loudly

Cue 4   Black-out   (Page 25)
           Girls' choir singing "All Things Bright and Beautiful"

Cue 5   The Lights come up   (Page 25)
           Fade girls' choir singing. Clock strikes six

Cue 6   **Miss Fisher**: "…going to do, D'Vere?"   (Page 31)
           Handbell ringing

Cue 7   The Lights slowly fade   (Page 35)
           Girls' choir singing "What a Friend We Have in Jesus"

ACT II

Cue 8   To open   (Page 36)
           Clock strikes eight

Cue 9   **Miss Duke**: "…cheerful about all this."   (Page 46)
           Hand bell ringing

Cue 10   **Miss Kyte**: "…we all expected it to fall."   (Page 60)
           Clock strikes nine